Efficient Management
of Large Metadata Catalogs in a Ubiquitous Computing Environment

DANIEL BEATTY

authorHOUSE®

AuthorHouse™
1663 Liberty Drive
Bloomington, IN 47403
www.authorhouse.com
Phone: 1 (800) 839-8640

Published by AuthorHouse 04/27/2019

ISBN: 978-1-5462-6538-2 (sc)
ISBN: 978-1-5462-6537-5 (e)

Library of Congress Control Number: 2018912684

Print information available on the last page.

Any people depicted in stock imagery provided by Getty Images are models, and such images are being used for illustrative purposes only. Certain stock imagery © Getty Images.

This book is printed on acid-free paper.

Because of the dynamic nature of the Internet, any web addresses or links contained in this book may have changed since publication and may no longer be valid. The views expressed in this work are solely those of the author and do not necessarily reflect the views of the publisher, and the publisher hereby disclaims any responsibility for them.

CONTENTS

Acknowledgements... vii

Abstract.. ix

List of Tables... xi

List of Figures xiii

1 Introduction 1

    1.1   Motivation 1

    1.2   Key Concepts.. 2

        1.2.1   Data Mining.. 2

        1.2.2   Observations... 2

        1.2.3   Definitions of Cloud Computing.. 3

    1.3   Problem Statement 4

    1.4   Solution Approach.. 5

2 Background Information 7

    2.1   Observations and Calibrations 7

    2.2   Distribution Dependent Tools 8

    2.3   Integration of Content Management.. 9

    2.4   Modern Web Architecture Applied to Metadata Catalogs 10

    2.5   Synchronizing Data Sets 12

    2.6   Metadata In Cloud Computing 12

3 Content Management Architecture... 14

    3.1   Comparing Observed Objects to Observations 14

    3.2   Bridging Relational Databases to Object-Oriented Models 15

    3.3   Building Web Responses with Models and Actions.. 18

    3.4   Revised Image Query Service (RIQS) 18

    3.5   Revised Image Query Service (RIQS) Illustration 20

4 A Mobile Code Architecture.. 23

    4.1   Data Models For A Generic Photographic Observation Catalog..................... 23

    4.2   Mapping Observed Objects back to Observations... 25

    4.3   Marshaling a Catalog Archive Service... 27

        4.3.1   Marshaling... 27

        4.3.2   Overhead Analysis 27

        4.3.3   An Improved Marshaling Structure. 28

    4.4   Building a Mobile Agent 29

5 Rule-based Context Management Architecture... 32

    5.1   Obtaining Access To The Observation Sources 32

        5.1.1   The File Structure Established in the Early Data Release of the Sloan
                Digital Sky Survey... 33

        5.1.2   Archive Access through Business Logic and Component Actions.......... 35

            5.1.2.1   Target Selection Segment 36

5.1.2.2   Target Selection Fields 37

5.1.2.3   Z Emission and Cross Correlation 37

5.1.2.3   Spectral Inventory.. 37

5.1.2.4   Spectral Object Family of Tables.. 37

5.1.2.5   Plate Object Table 38

5.1.2.6   Quasar Sample Object 38

5.2   Rule Based and Context Oriented Response Factory............................ 38

5.2.1   Rules and Engines.. 39

5.2.2   Context Management 40

5.2.3   Attribute Level Components.. 40

5.2.4   Default Behavior.. 40

5.2.5   Flow Control 41

5.3   Rule Based Request and Response... 41

5.4   Experiments 43

5.5   Results 45

6   Representational State Transfer Architecture 51

6.1   A Model for Photographs Taken By Spectroscopes 51

6.1.1   Spectral Domain Model... 51

6.1.2   Joining the Photographic Model 52

6.2   Dynamic Tabular Data About The Night Sky In A Relational Database 56

6.2.1   Object-Relational Friendly Virtual Observation Tables.................. 56

6.2.2   General Table Migration 60

6.3   Ubiquity by Representation 60

6.3.1   Mapping Network Addresses to Survey Entities............................. 62

6.3.2   Another Marshaling Layer System 62

6.4   Migrating The Sloan Digital Sky Survey.. 63

6.4.1   Proxy Application To Unorganized Dataset 64

6.4.2   Synchronizing Application-Interface 64

7   Conclusions 71

Bibliography... 73

Efficient Management of Large Metadata Catalogs
in a Distributed Computing Environment

Daniel D. Beatty

Ph.D. Student

Texas Tech University

Lubbock, TX 79409

ACKNOWLEDGEMENTS

I wish to acknowledge the help and support of my family: both my mother (Ann) and grandfather (the late Rev. David Herman). They have both been there for me during these challenging efforts associated with the doctoral program. For example, my family has helped by relieving expenses that were not otherwise planned or budgeted. Life is full of matters that we both plan for and those we fail to plan for. My family exercised these acts of mercy and ensured that these unexpected troubles were not catastrophic. My grandfather was also a mentor and source of great encouragement that has inspired me throughout the program. May my grandfather rest in peace, and my gratitude for all he did for me be known.

During the program, one of the un-budgeted and unplanned for events included injuries sustained in 2008 and 2010. As a disabled American veteran, I have become accustom to overcome weaknesses imposed by injuries. I had considered them part of the cost of achievement. Although some injuries require more help than I could manage on my own. In 2008, the medical personnel of University Medical Center and Texas Tech Medical were there to assist me, as well as friends, committee members, and clergy. Likewise in 2010 to present, medical personnel in Ridgecrest, California helped tremendously. Extreme pain and injury can ruin a life and destroy excellence before it is accomplished. Physicians like Dr. George Perdikis and Dr. William Mouradian and therapist such as Katherine Garcia and Parth Patel have done a tremendous job in the field of pain management. Similarly, a number of pastors and professionals of the spirit provided me guidance during these trials of pain. These professionals included Rev. Brian Dupree, Rev. Tim Radkey, Rev. Jay Beyer, and Rev. William Lindenmeyer. This management and guidance has made a critical difference by enabling me to keep working on this research despite searing pain, and bring it to fruition in the form of this dissertation. These people have my heart felt gratitude.

Also during the program, I had received four Apple World Wide Developer Conference (WWDC) scholarships, and I had presented posters at 3 WWDC events. What was more valuable was the training and technical guidance I received from many fellow participants at the WWDC that provided insight and ideas that influenced the direction of this research. It is believed that I would not received such guidance from any place on earth pertaining to these subjects. There were people like Chuck Hill of Global Village Consulting, Mark Ritchie, David Ress (Ph.D.) of General Dynamics, David Leber, and Mike Schrag. To each of these gentlemen who helped me, and the countless others in the Apple and WebObjects Communities that provided me wisdom on these topics, thank you.

ABSTRACT

Trends in experimental sciences, such as astrophysics, have led to many critically needed, non-normalized, and massive meta-data catalogs that organize collections of recorded photographic and spectrographic observations of similar size. Observations of the night sky can best be presented using a data model that conveys the observations, analysis, objects contained with the observations, and results of analysis pertaining to those objects. Such a model is proposed and it is referred to as the internet Flexible Image Transport System (iFITS). In addition, a set of mapping functions to transform instances of the Sloan Digital Sky Survey into instances of iFITS, a light-weight marshaling method to transfer data to and from server side instances to mobile instances. Furthermore, this dissertation explores four architectures such as content management, software/ infrastructure/ platform as a service, context rule engine based request-response loop factory, and representational state transfer (REST) based query engines to facilitate the mining of the meta-data catalogs containing these observations.

LIST OF TABLES

6.1   Network Actions Mapping to Controller Actions 62

LIST OF FIGURES

Figure 1   Photographic Observation Image Table Component 19

Figure 2   EO Modeler Transformation 20

Figure 3   User selected section of the sky with selection form and one observation. 21

Figure 4   Observation Class Stucture 23

Figure 5   Gadget Object UML 30

Figure 6   Fire Mashup Default 31

Figure 7   This diagram was taken from David Leber's World Wide WebObjects
            Developer's Conference (WOWODC) 2009 session on Direct to Web. 39

Figure 8   Rule Based Revised Image Query Service Query Page 44

Figure 9   The Best Target Selection Field Query Result List 45

Figure 10   Brute Force Memory Load Delivery Times for the Measured Lines from
            selected trials. 47

Figure 11   Load Times for the Table Line Ratios from selected trials............................ 48

Figure 12   Spectral Object Times 49

Figure 13   Memory Footprint.. 50

Figure 14   iFITS with Spectral Observations.. 53

Figure 15   Non ORM friendly Version of Table Object 55

Figure 16   Tabular Observation.. 57

Figure 17   The iFITS Structure without Attachments 59

Figure 18   REST Handling and Marshaling Engine reverse engineered from the Ruby/
            WOnder REST engine (Project WOnder's implementation)................................. 61

Figure 19   Mobile Shoebox application representation. 65

Figure 20   Structure for a Registration Resource 67

Figure 21   Process for retrieving pushed request nodes 68

Figure 22   Full Update Action for the Slow Change Exchange.................................... 69

Figure 23   Model for Synchronizing Change Sets.. 70

CHAPTER 1

INTRODUCTION

This research project addresses issues related to managing large repositories, the data observed and recorded within, and meta-data; compare results from multiple sources; and provide expandability that can and does enlist 3rd party tools. The work proposed is part of a larger a project started at Texas Tech University under the Distributed Computing Lab called Sky Raider. Sky Raider should expand on this work to provide collaborative support between many catalogs, and provide an unifying catalog that can be used by many investigators to warehouse their observations and analysis.

Section 1 Motivation

Chris Stoughton with the Sloan Digital Sky Survey (Szalay, Gray et al. 2001) proposed to port the Data Release 1 (DR1) to Texas Tech in 2003. A copy of the database, raw data files, and web program interface were ported to TTU as described in (Hegde 2004). Later, additional hardware was acquired to house the massive database.

DR1 consists of four major parts. One part consists of a meta-data catalog contained in a database. A second part is a massive collection of raw data files. A, third part consist of a web program to deliver data files based on query requests. A fourth part is a collage maker that would join prepared images such that it appeared to be one big observation of the night sky.

The web program and the collage maker are Fermi National Accelerator Laboratory (FNAL) products of the SDSS project. These products were interwoven, and very difficult to separate. Furthermore, they were highly dependent on libraries contained in FNAL's distribution of Linux. This distribution of DR1 tools was the only place where these packages could be found and run.

After the mirror project reached its completion, the machine housing the web program and collage maker reached obsolescence and failed. This had the effect of crippling access to the DR1 mirror. Yet, the database and data files remained in storage available for further research. This prompted the idea to design and develop a new web interface.

The Sky Raider Project was created to address the flaws in this system and devise a mechanism that would achieve the objectives of the SDSS. It was originally envisioned that other astronomers and fellow scientists would contribute to the SDSS with analysis and observations of their own. The SDSS collaboration made subsequent catalog releases. However, the design of DR1 and subsequent releases essentially created considerable barriers from any other contributors. Thus, Sky Raider was created to facilitate the contributions from astronomers and provide tools to analyze those contributions.

So why is astronomical data so difficult? This phenomenon is not limited to astronomy, and applies to each scientific discipline. A trend exists across a majority of the scientific disciplines to construct a database schema with very little analysis on the concepts being represented. This leads to databases with tables with an enormous set of attributes.

This dissertation describes the first results of the Sky Raider project. This project incorporates the framework of cloud computing, considers new design principles, and addresses key necessary features to expand access capabilities to DR1 along with other releases and catalogs. Furthermore, we propose a new catalog that can be of service to every astronomer and scientist in the world.

Section 2 Key Concepts

Sub-Section 1 Data Mining

Some definitions of data mining as written in (Ian H. Wittman 2005) claim its purpose is to close the gap of generating knowledge and understanding such knowledge. Machine learning (Jiawei Han 2006) claims that data mining includes association, classification and clustering. The notion of association is applicable to goal states, rule refinement and a-monotonic logic. Classification and clustering is a notion based on patterns of approximation and statistics.

The focus of this work is on metadata catalogs, which are inherently a form of data warehousing. A data warehouse generalizes and consolidates data in a multidimensional space (Jiawei Han 2006). Such a data warehouse makes data mining possible since it maintains such data for on-line analytical processing (OLAP). The fundamental data mining techniques of association, classification, prediction, and clustering can be integrated with OLAP. It can be argued that an Object Relational Mapping (ORM) engine can provide the facilities of OLAP serving as a fundamental framework where data mining functions can be applied.

For data mining techniques to be meaningful, the data must be meet certain relevancy conditions such as context and scale. If two database tables have a valid mapping to an intermediary table where the contexts are equivalent and the same scale can be applied, then data mining algorithms have meaning. To accomplish this, there has to be a common structure and a mapping function between the two database tables.

This work brings forth a new structure that can be applied to learn much about astronomy. This structure provides a basic syntax to reference facts collected pertaining to the night sky and describe knowledge generated from those facts. Furthermore, this set of mapping functions are devised to compare another sky catalog. This work is applicable to metadata catalogs in general by providing a possible standard for constructing an intermediate catalog that can potentially facilitate OLAP functionality.

Sub-Section 2 Observations

In this dissertation, three types of observations are described and serve as a basis for knowledge discovery: namely mono-wavelength, spectral, and tabular. Mono-wavelength observations are commonly called photographic observations. Spectroscopic and photographic observations are captured by Charged Coupled Device (CCD) arrays as described in (Howell 2000) and the type of observations defines the meaning of each CCD element. Analysis on these observations reveal sources of interest such as stars, nebulae, galaxies, or quasars noticed in the recorded case. Tabular observations have been recorded for centuries in one form or another. Tabular observations involve a record of descriptions, definitions, references, and a mapping of attributes with iterations to show results. In this work, a structure that can represent each of the observation types and knowledge learned from them is proposed. This structure in its own right is possibly a new standard for representing astronomical data and metadata catalogs at large.

Sub-Section 3 Definitions of Cloud Computing

The term *Cloud Computing* has been closely associated with terms such as on-demand computing, software as a service, and (an/the) internet as a platform. These terms have also been used to describe Grid computing.

The Berkeley View of Cloud Computing (Armbrust, Fox et al. 2009) states

> "*Cloud computing* refers to both, the applications delivered as services over the Internet, and the hardware and systems software in the data-centers that provide those services."

This definition acknowledges two key notions of Cloud computing:

- Software can and is provided as a service.

- Cloud services provide this software through an arrangement of hardware and system software running at datacenter facilities.

The Berkeley View is not new. Distributed computing has considered concepts of virtualization, transparent access, and scalability for decades as noted in (Hayes 2008). The Berkeley View definition acknowledges that applications and systems can be supplied virtually, and therefore provide the illusion of infinite computing resources that are available on demand.

The Berkeley View is not the only definition of *cloud computing*. A second definition of *cloud computing* described in (Hayes 2008) emphasizes the notion of an *Infrastructure as a Service*. Infrastructure providers provide vast storage and computing capacity. The purpose of this is to grow or shrink resources to fit the needs and budgets of those who consume this storage.

Both (Armbrust, Fox et al. 2009) and (Hayes 2008) surveyed a third concept of *cloud computing* known as *platform as a service*. In this case, virtual computing platforms are provided on demand. These platforms may in turn provide software as a service. From this perspective, the service attempts to provide a load balanced, dynamically provisioned, and notion of unified computing resource.

A fourth definition proposed in (Vaquero, Rodero-Merino et al. 2009) states:

> "Clouds are large pools of easily usable and accessible virtualized resources (such as hardware, development platforms, and/ or services). These resources can be dynamically reconfigured to adjust to a variable load (scale), allowing also for an optimum resource utilization. This pool of resources is typically exploited by a pay-per-use model that are offered by the Infrastructure Provider by means of customized Service Level Agreements."

Each of these definitions entail a set of characteristics that are associated with the cloud computing model. The cloud computing model includes on-demand self-service, capabilities are provided over network where access is available to a broad array of platforms, resources are pooled, capabilities can rapidly be provisioned in an elastic fashion, and service is measurable. In addition, several common deployment models have emerged. These include private, community, public deployments and there are hybrids amongst these deployment types. This different deployment types, service models, and essential characteristics provide the basis for the following definition specified in (Mell and Grance 2011)

> "Cloud computing is a model for enabling ubiquitous, convenient, on-demand network access to a shared pool of configurable computing resources (e.g., networks, servers, storage, applications, and services) that can be rapidly provisioned and released with minimal management effort or service provider interaction. This cloud model is composed of five essential characteristics, three service models, and four deployment models."

The work proposed uses mobile agents, local clients, and datacenter resources to facilitate the querying, managing, and analyzing of multiple sources. These mobile agents broker the services that provide these sources. The local client may also provide resources such as persistent storage and computational capabilities. Each datacenter may supply either a source knowledge or computational resource. Thus, the work proposed addresses querying multiple large repositories in a non-trivial way within the *cloud computing* paradigm as stated in (Vaquero, Rodero-Merino et al. 2009). The implication of these key concepts and the architecture(s) proposed leads to a possible standard to access not only sky survey data, but also other large data catalogs such as medical images, geological data, bioinformatics, and military catalog applications.

Section 3 Problem Statement

The primary objective of the Sloan Digital Sky Survey catalog (York 2000) is to "support detailed investigations of the distributions of luminous and non-nonluminous matter in the Universe." These investigations imply a large metadata catalog in order to reference sources of this matter. Most of these sources are astronomical phenomena such as stars, quasars, nebulae, and galaxies.

None of the data releases of the Sloan Digital Sky Survey ever had a well-organized structure, such as described in (Ullman 1988), applied to their metadata catalog. Studies such as (Qiusheng, Wang et al. 2007) and (Hernandez 2009) indicate that knowledge base / database system are better organized when tables have a small number of attributes and tables exploit relationships. Each of the data releases have the opposite, which includes unrelated tables to reference each source observed and associated analysis results obtained through calibration procedures.

Furthermore, there are other surveys and astronomers who collect observations from remote places. These places have the advantage of low light pollution. The tradeoff is that they have a low communication capability to the internet and its resources.

Furthermore, current catalog schemes have barriers in common that limit sharing facts and findings. Current procedures imply that the information gathered is complete, ready for publication, and one has the money to sponsor a new survey with a new catalog. Each new catalog produced prior to the one introduced here indeed represents a burden in determining a scheme to represent the data collected, the storage facility, and engines to retrieve that data.

Therefore, this work presents the following corollary: given a data set; the purpose of that dataset; and concepts of observations, cloud computing, and content management there exists an efficient structure that can be a standard for similar subject dataset(s), a mapping mechanism to incorporate these other datasets held in distinct metadata catalogs, and a virtual appliance - mashup hybrid that can automate the facade to use these disparate datasets in the same metric and scale. Determining the validity of this corollary and applying to SDSS DR1 dataset allows the SDSS objective to be fulfilled by capturing the essence of astronomical observation with mobile collections, analysis, and collaborative sharing amongst astronomers who may operate in remote areas. The low cost solution to show this corollary is non-trivial. There are architectural considerations to manage the limitations of cloud computing to ensure that the virtual appliance solution can scale well in the face of high demand.

Section 4 Solution Approach

In order to meet these challenges, a combination of four basic architectures and one evolving structure are explored. The implementations of some of these architectures are considered emerging technologies. Examination of these architectures shall consider concept and effectiveness toward achieving the challenge goals. Each prototype evaluation is based on metrics pertinent to both mobile and portable devices designed to operate in remote areas such as bandwidth, latency, speed, and power consumption. Each structure is examined to determine how effectively it captures the astronomical data of DR1 and possibly other catalogs. This process should reveal which combination of these architectures and structures provide a satisfactory basis for a prototype that can fulfill the SDSS objective while making such a catalog practical for every astronomer.

Chapter 2 provides literature review on astronomical catalogs, their analysis tools, and general content management. Also included are backgrounds on cloud computing and meta-data management in a distributed environment.

The first of these architectures is a server side web application utilizing content management techniques. This architecture is presented in Chapter 3. This architecture exhibits building blocks that are used to retrieve the Data Release 1 catalog data and related source files. Some work has already been accomplished by demonstrating and evaluating this architecture. This work was published in (Beatty and Lopez-Benitez 2009).

A second architecture, described in Chapter 4, adds a mashup to the server side web application. This Mashup - Server Side web application hybrid exhibits additional building blocks such as marshaling, restructuring, and user interface (UI) manipulation to achieve the illusion of a structure suited to astronomical observations. Some work has also been performed on examining this architecture and the results of this work was published in (Beatty and Lopez-Benitez 2010).

The third of these architectures is an emerging technology based on the notion of a factory governed context and a rule set. Since this architecture is currently implemented by only one framework, it bears the name of that framework "Direct to Web"[1]. This architecture is described in Chapter 5 by examination of Project Wonder's open source implementation.

The fourth architecture is also an emerging technology, known as RESTful Web Services. This type of architecture accepts queries based on paths in the REST architecture described in (Fielding 2000). There is an architecture derived from both the factory design pattern and RESTful

---

[1] Trademark of Apple, Inc.

Web Services architecture that is commonly called "RESTful Resource Routes" and "RESTful Refactoring of Resources Using CRUD" in (Cashion 2007). This architecture is examined from a source implementation in Java provided by Project Wonder[2]. Chapter 6 examines this architecture and the ability to map different structures together either directly or by a mobile proxy application.

The evolving structure is described in Chapter 6 Section 1 and Chapter 6 Section 2 . This structure has been named the internet Flexible Image Transport System (iFITS). Each version adds a different type of observations and makes relations to sources that reveal the type of observation. A mapping of the original DR1 to these structures is illustrated in Chapter 5 Section 1 Sub-Section 2 . With this mapping and a combination of the four architectures, a prototype emerges that is a potential solution to the stated challenges. Some work on this structure has already been presented along with the second architecture in (Beatty and Lopez-Benitez 2010).

The contribution described includes structure design, the mashup mobile agent, combination of these architectures, and lastly a restructuring mechanism that allows multiple catalog types to be unified despite the separation. This contribution has the potential of meeting the expectations of the stated challenges. Furthermore, the evaluation of these contributions is in and of itself another contribution to determine effectiveness and efficiency of this architecture combination at meeting the expectations of the stated challenges. Both the third and fourth architecture have the potential of addressing malformed database structures and applications. In some cases, addressing these challenges means providing a new interface for the malformed structure. In other cases, addressing these challenges means mapping and migrating the data into a much more organized structure. Lastly, the prototype itself can be seen as a contribution to both the observer and analyst searching for "detailed investigations of the distributions of luminous and non-luminous matter in the Universe."

---

[2] http://webobjects.mdimension.com/hudson/job/Wonder54/javadoc/er/rest/package-summary.html

CHAPTER 2

BACKGROUND INFORMATION

DR1 recorded information into many tables. These tables are thoroughly examined in Chapter 5 Section 1 . Some tables were written as notes about the observation itself. These records served as both a list to determine which observations to take and reference for how the observation was obtained. Other tables were derived from analysis of the observations.

DR1 consists of a large collection of observation files and a metadata catalog stored on a MySQL database. The observations were stored and cataloged by mapping the sky into stripes (The SDSS collaboration 2003), where photographs of the night sky could be organized. Each photograph from the telescope was acquired by a Charged Coupled Device (CCD) camera and stored in Flexible Image Transport System (FITS) (Wells, Greisen et al. 1981) and (Hanisch and et.al. 2001) formatted files. Each stripe was organized into a directory structure of *run*, rerun, camera column, and *f*ields referred to as the Observed Object Critical Attributes and as part of the metadata catalog serve to organize these images. Note that both the photographic and spectral observations have references to these critical attributes. Furthermore, these attributes can be used to construct the location of the original observations by SDSS' own scheme.

One special characteristic about the Spectral Object table is that it also includes attributes to the right ascension (α) and declination (δ). Those attributes are amongst the most common queried in order to obtain observations and meta-data from most catalogs. Often, a range of values of varying geometries are applied to these attributes to obtain a set of observations.

Sky Raider inherits the observations and calibrations of SDSS DR1, with the lessons learned from establishing DR1's mirror. These lessons included how to share and distribute tools to analyze observations. Sky Raider has also benefited from the application of content management techniques to rebuild the mirror of DR1 whose services rival the existing DR7 service.

Section 1 Observations and Calibrations

Just as important as the effort to acquire observations of the night sky, are the methods to calibrate those observations. These methods are used by both computer vision and astronomical communities to compare images either taken by the same or different instruments to determine facts of common features. Analyzing photographic observations include photometric, stamp, astrometric and image calibrations. Spectroscopy adds a set of calibrations to establish a scale for the measurement of wavelength versus photon flux.

For photometric observations, analysis starts with data reduction tools for *d*ark fields, *b*ias fields, *f*lat fields, and *n*oise fields. Each of these fields are well known in the CCD astronomical literature (Howell 2000) and (Kitchin 2003). These fields are quantifiable properties of the observation instruments and environment where each measurement was made. Each field, except for the noise field, can be, and often is, compared against a standard measurement taken by the instrument prior to observations to ensure that conditions of the instrument can be compared later. The noise field has three components for which the most significant is noise from the signal (source) itself. In the case of the SDSS, calibrations were performed by comparing known standards provided by the US Naval Observatory and observations obtained by SDSS' instrument of the same source object. Also, SDSS referenced neighboring color cells for each source to validate an observation. Thus the fields were determined indirectly.

A postage stamp analysis uses centroids of bright stars and compares these objects position with that of expected positions for the same object. These values contribute to computing the point spread functions (PSF) as a function of position across each frame (The SDSS collaboration 2003).

In addition to photometric calibration, SDSS made astrometric observations taken at the same time as the photometric observations (from a set of CCD cells arranged along the width of the camera.) This technique references the Tycho and Hipparacos catalogues (York 2000). Further references are made with *FIRST* catalog as referenced (Croft, de Vries et al. 2007) and *2MASS* catalogs as shown in (Glikman, Helfand et al. 2007) and (Cutri, Skrutskie et al. 2003) to establish accuracy of the astrometric calibration and observation. This observation combined with results of the postage stamp pipeline yields an astrometric calibration. It is this calibration that allows detected objects to be matched against J2000 catalog coordinates as reported in (Ochsenbein, Bauer et al. 2000) (Urban, Corbin et al. 1998).

Lastly, the imaging calibration corrects raw frames from instrumental effects, detects objects on the corrected frames, correlates matching objects from different filters, de-blends overlapping objects, and measures parameters for the objects. The imaging calibration is dependent on the astrometric calibration.

Modern astronomical spectroscopic observations inherit many of the reductions necessary for photographic observations since the final recording mechanism is the same. Both spectrographic and photographic observations are a CCD image. The difference is the presence of a light separation mechanism such as a prism, grating, or hybrid construction described in (Kitchin 2003). Thus, the photometric reductions are inherently necessary to standardize spectroscopic images, as well. A similar technique to postage stamping applies to spectroscopic observations to identify features and arrange noise filtration. An astrometric observation is typically made from a telescope parallel to the spectroscopic telescope. The calibration of the astrometric observation have a different value as the reference to the known objects in that observation. These references are used to standardize spectrographic readings.

Section 2 Distribution Dependent Tools

SDSS built a set of tools later designated Astrotools and Dervish to compute its calibrations, as noted in (Tucker and et.al. 2006). By SDSS DR2, much of the functionality of Astrotools (also referred to as FNAL Dervish) was attempted on grids such as Condor (Nieto-Santisteban, Szalay et al. 2005). These calculations included spatial information, image processing, photometric processing, and feature detection.

Similarly, two other sets of tools for astronomical image reduction also existed at the time as Dervish. NASA had published a standard tool called FITSIO shown in (Pence 1995). It was a FORTRAN code to translate FITS data into structure that could be used by user built tools. Some of these tools were incorporated and provided by NASA as published in (Pence 1992). Other tools were distributed and fostered through many observatories and universities. One of these toolsets is Image Reduction and Analysis Facility (IRAF) as shown in (Tody 1993) and another was SAO Image's products as published in (Howell 2000) and (Lewis and Bridger 2006).

Each tool set is capable of performing reductions to achieve each of these calibrations. Dervish was used by SDSS since it was conveniently constructed in-house, and could be modified to suit the purposes of any FNAL project. Similarly, other projects have used either straight NASA tools or derived versions such as IRAF. IRAF and DS9 each have a wide distribution in the astronomical community, abundance of documentation, and wealth of institutions providing training on each of these tools.

There are not many publications on Dervish. It is possible to reverse-engineer the copy supplied to Texas Tech in the DR1 mirror. Unfortunately, that code was made with many dependencies contained only in the FNAL distribution of Linux.

FITSIO is available on each platform. Both IRAF and DS9 conveniently organize the NASA libraries into tasks that are made for both analysis and classic academic lab exercises. Therefore, this dissertation considers a task to build services for the retrieval and analysis mechanisms of DS9. IRAF and DS9 was chosen primarily due to its well documented collection of tools. It is described in many journals and books such as (Howell 2000) as being commonly used in academic environments and thus provides a reproducible and verifiable standard.

The Infrared Processing and Analysis Center[3] supply a catalog called 2MASS through a mechanism called General Catalog Query Engine (GATOR) as described in (Pasquali, Kauffmann et al. 2005) and (Briukhov, Kalinichenko et al. 2005). Data is queried in these cases through a service called CatQuery[4]. Each query is keyword coded with a set of parameters such as *main*, *spatial*, *catalog*, *output format*, *description*, *order*, *constraint*, and *on list*[5]. The output of these queries have many forms including the VO Table (Williams and et.al. 2004) developed by and for the International Virtual Observatory Alliance. DS9 consumes these services through a web access mechanism shown in (Padovani 1998) and (Cutri, Skrutskie et al. 2003). This mechanism follows a trend known as Representational State Transfer (REST) services as described in (Fielding 2000).

Section 3 Integration of Content Management

The work proposed makes use of content management techniques as well many different design patterns. A content management system (CMS) governs the contributions of original, derived, or revised information components via tools that collect, analyze, revise, and organize such contributions, as explained in (Nakano 2001). Many other definitions require control of the tools themselves and associate a CMS with the World Wide Web (WWW). A CMS inherently requires some form of network support to supply its tools and content to multiple users, institutions and/or machines.

Most active content and portal systems (Aronsson 2002) consist of source writing features to provide links, text formatting, and methods to organize such sources. Some of these systems (Marshall

---

[3] joint venture of the Division of Physics, Mathematics and Astronomy at Caltech, and the Space and Earth Sciences Program Directorate at JPL NASA

[4] http://irsa.ipac.caltech.edu/cgi-bin/Gator/nph-query

[5] http://irsa.ipac.caltech.edu/applications/Gator/GatorAid/catsearch.html

2006) have been more successful than others. Notable elements in these systems include an editor, simple mechanisms for user authentication and authoring content, and search and sharing methods.

For earth-bound locations, the concept of locating astronomical objects by name is the reciprocal query to a geographical information system (GIS) search. Usually, astronomical catalogs reference a set of sky coordinates for a given name, which are used to aim a telescope (Ashford 2006) and (di Cicco 2006).

Design patterns, such as bridging, facade, visitor, and model-view-control (MVC) paradigm (Gamma, Helm et al. 1994) define a flexible framework within which CMS can be used. For example, the bridging design pattern is applied to the meta-data catalog and the query service view, which have no evolution in common except to work together. Therefore, bridging these two classes by a common interface defines a CM technique that has led to a flexible and expandable content manager described later.

Likewise, applying the facade design pattern to objects obtained from the meta-data catalog produces a model applicable to referencing images. For example, a photographic observation contains many source objects that are captured by the imaging device. In order to reference a photographic observation by coordinates in the sky, one references the source objects by coordinates. Two of DR1's tables reference the photographic observation itself, *Fields* and *segments*. There is no photographic observation table containing reference to sky coordinates in DR1, but the Spectral Object Table does and has one-to-one correspondence with objects in the photographic observations. Thus each object is referenced from the Spectral Object Table and can be selected for special observation by instruments like a spectroscope. A *b*ridging-facade is needed to bridge the observation as a structure with references to each object in Spectral Object Tables, providing flexibility for the content manager.

An Object Relational Mapper (ORM) supplies a bridging facade between the database adaptor and data model that allows each database model, table, row, and relationship to be treated as a set of managed objects. A system that implements patterns on a multiple user, client-server basis is called an Enterprise Object Relational Management/ Mapping System. A mature implementation of an Enterprise ORM System is provided by Apple's *WebObjects*(WO) (Paine 1997), and the framework that supplies the ORM is called *E*nterprise Objects (EO) (Marinescu 2006) and (Galbraith, Maric et al. 2001). Combining WO and EO with the set of design patterns mentioned lead to a flexible web application applied to DR1 image retrieval and provides the backbone of RIQS.

Many architectures have been proposed for catalogs of astronomical surveys. Some have considered some notions of content management. These considerations include the design patterns described. Other considerations include close examinations of the SDSS Catalog Archive Service (CAS) structure. Each of a consideration contributed to evolving forms of the Revised Image Query Service (RIQS).

Section 4 Modern Web Architecture Applied to Metadata Catalogs

Representational State Transfer (REST) as defined in (Fielding and Taylor 2000), (Fielding 2000), and (Fielding, Software et al. 2002) is an abstraction of architectural elements within a hypermedia system, and at its most basic level can be defined in terms of resource URLs and component action verbs. According to (Fielding, Software et al. 2002), the world wide web itself is an instance of REST architecture. The four main action verbs supported by HTTP include *GET*, *PUT*, *POST*, and *DELETE*.

There is also an architecture that works well with basic combinations of ORM and CRUD as shown in (Brandon 2002) and (Armour and Miller 2001). These combinations form the basis for many modern ORM interface implementations including Microsoft's XQuery and LINQ ((Barla, Bartalos et al. 2007)), Apple's *Web*Objects and *C*ore Data as described in (Beatty and Lopez-Benitez 2010) and (Beatty and Lopez-Benitez 2009), and Ruby on Rails as described in (Zeng, Chen et al. 2005, Geer 2006, Bachle and Kirchberg 2007, Li, Chen et al. 2007)..

The modern web architecture employs connector called a resolver. A *r*esolver, as defined by (Fielding, Software et al. 2002), "translates a partial or complete resource identifier into a network address information needed to establish an inter-component connection." A new architecture is emerging that applies the resolver to connect components implementing CRUD operations such as described in (Cashion 2007, Richardson and Ruby 2007, Forcier, Bissex et al. 2008, Sandoval 2009, Wang and Fan 2009). Implementations of this new architecture leads to the emergence of a new technology called *R*ESTful Web Services as documented in (Pautasso, Zimmermann et al. 2008, Pautasso 2009, Nowak, Pautasso et al. 2010).

There is a form of *R*ESTful Web Service that is emerging amongst ORM driven applications. This variation combines an extended notion of model, view, and controller (MVC) architectures and adds notions of routes, formatters, and key-filters. A *R*ESTful Web Service implemented in this manner can be called a *r*esource-controlled architecture. The purpose of each component is defined as follows:

- An *e*diting context, typically but not always supplied by an ORM, provides persistent instances contained in an application.

- A *r*esource is ORM entity, provision, some subject, or object provided by the RESTful Web Service that can be drawn upon and acted on by consumers and with *r*outes has the notion of a complete linguistic sentence.

- A *r*esource route (or *r*oute for short) is the portion of a resource that provides mapping between REST resource identifiers (URL) and action verb combinations to CRUD component actions.

- A *f*ormatter provides marshaling from each object type in the editing context to each marshaling format type supported.

- A *k*ey-filter governs the attributes and relations that marshaled from the entities.

- A *c*ontroller implements the CRUD actions. Each controller parses each request and formats each response.

An example of an astronomical catalog that employees RESTful Web Services has been developed by the Infrared Processing and Analysis Center (IPAC)[6]. The IPAC supplies a catalog called 2MASS

---

[6] joint venture of the Division of Physics, Mathematics and Astronomy at Caltech, and the Space and Earth Sciences Program Directorate at JPL NASA

through a mechanism called General Catalog Query Engine (GATOR) as described in (Briukhov, Kalinichenko et al. 2005, Pasquali, Kauffmann et al. 2005). Data is queried in these cases through a service called CatQuery[7]. Each query is keyword coded with a set of parameters such as *main*, *spatial*, *catalog*, *output format*, *description*, *order*, *constraint*, and *on list*[8]. The output of these queries have many forms including the VO Table developed by (Williams and et.al. 2004) and for the International Virtual Observatory Alliance. Astronomers and their analysis tools consume these services through a RESTful Web Service described in (Padovani 1998, Cutri, Skrutskie et al. 2003).

Section 5 Synchronizing Data Sets

Delta-Grid was envisioned to address semantic correctness of concurrent process execution. These issues include undo, redo, and recovery operations for RDBMS systems. For example, a Delta-Enabled Grid Service is one approach to resolving service execution failure, service recovery, and concurrent process interference based on read and write dependency tracking for service execution. This type of resolution has been implemented by Oracle's stream and process history capture system.

Recovery of failed processes and synchronization are related topics. A process may succeed in one process and not be reflected in the whole system for one reason. Therefore, synchronization also requires the notion of these delta's. This work takes a similar approach, but through an ORM. Many ORM's supply notification systems similar to Oracle's streams, and these can be used to construct process history capture systems (PHCS) similar to those used in DEGS. In the synchronization case, the PHCS is shared with each node (mobile or shoe-box) that has copy of the entity being tracked.

While there is much similarity between these two topics, the focus of this work is not the deltas exclusively. Rather, these delta systems serve as a means to an end. The means they provide is part of a transport, map, and marshal system designed to help translate unorganized sets into organized equivalents.

Section 6 Metadata In Cloud Computing

Pioneers for organizing and providing metadata include SAM, Gryphn, SDSS, and many others. Each group (such as (Pordes, Trumbo et al. 2001, Deelman, Kesselman et al. 2002, Rajasekar, Wan et al. 2002, Hanisch and et.al. 2003, Santos and Koblitz 2006)) credit toolkits such as Globus and more specifically GridFTP. In a weather example, (Chervenak, Deelman et al. 2003), the issues are getting the data out with request managers and heavy data transfers. Many common web browsers have caught up by incorporating the heavy data transfer mechanisms in to their structure, such as (Meyer 2008, Hernandez 2009). In other cases, there is a call for a hybrid.

Other metadata catalogs were inspired to handle music and the sale thereof. Some reports ((Aucouturier and Pachet 2002, Datta 2002, Keidl 2004)) show that these catalogs were to help preview the music so listeners would have a way to find songs they would like to buy. Some of the basic models for these catalogs have been used as examples for database courses. Each of these catalogs were anticipating millions of records for music titles and references to them. One of the most successful

---

[7] http://irsa.ipac.caltech.edu/cgi-bin/Gator/nph-query
[8] http://irsa.ipac.caltech.edu/applications/Gator/GatorAid/catsearch.html

and least documented case of audio-visual media metadata catalogs is iTunes[9] (both store and client application).

Some metadata oriented file system ideas are mentioned in context of cloud computing such as the *s*ector storage cloud (SSC) described in (Grossman, Gu et al. 2008). The SSC in particular claims to have distributed much of the SDSS data. However, it makes no mention of its meta-data catalog. The primary benefit for SSC is for its ability to store and transfer data, not the actual applying queries or searching for particular datasets. Thus, a solution is needed to convey the rich metadata originally contained in the SDSS catalog archive service (CAS), image query service (IQS) and spectral query service (SQS).

Geospatial grids such as (Lee and Percivall 2008) recognize the benefit to mobile devices and the use of standards. Most of these standards fit within the software as a service (SaaS) or infrastructure as a service (IaaS). However, platform as a service (PaaS) is ignored. There are many reasons to consider SaaS and IaaS for the file system or database provider. Namely, the resources required for the file system or database may be intensive and not easily portable. There are also reasons to consider PaaS. For example, PaaS is convenient for making copies of a catalog scheme so other survey's can have and use a catalog of their own. Also, PaaS is useful as an intermediary and a facade interface between a devices with special restrictions and services that would violate those restrictions. It is also reasonable to consider PaaS for ORM, Web Service, and mashup provision for such services.

Furthermore, there is a push in the ubiquitous computing community for query optimization and coordinating services for query data (Cuevas-Vicenttin, Vargas-Solar et al. 2009, Martinez-Medina, Bibineau et al. 2009). In both cases, the issues include conceptual issues such as mobility of the data/application, heterogeneous platforms, dynamically changing networks, data distribution, autonomy of data, value added services, and property list based dictionaries. These concepts focus on the query and not necessarily on the metadata catalog itself or access to it.

Mashups play a crucial role for metadata catalogs in ubiquitous computing at large and especially in mobile cases. Some definitions of a mashup documented in (Guo, Zhu et al. 2008) claim that "a Web mashup is defined as a Web page containing documents from different sources." Some ideas about mashups include the dissertation of an operating environment such as described in (Howell, Jackson et al. 2007). The criteria of different sources have been blatantly bent to suit development and web environments. Frameworks such as the Google Web Toolkit (Dewsbury 2007) claim that a mashup can simply be a mobile-code application typically implemented using Asynchronous JavaScript and XML (AJAX) that observes constraints determined by the principles of the same-origin policy, remote code inclusion, and can under certain constraints compose data from multiple web sites. This work acknowledges the relaxing of the multi-source requirement to illustrate concepts, and notes that the implementation of these concepts can act as components of such a multi-source mobile web application. Examples of the roles a mashup include both service broker architecture (SBA) and object relational mappers (ORM) to facilitate location oriented services ((Loreto, Mecklin et al. 2009)) and general query provisions such as in (Jarrar and Dikaiakos). The work described in this dissertation adds onto and includes these ideas.

---

[9] iTunes is a registered trademark of Apple, Inc.

CHAPTER 3

CONTENT MANAGEMENT ARCHITECTURE

Section 1 Comparing Observed Objects to Observations

Retrieving DR1 observations only requires six key attributes (*right* ascension (α), *declination* (δ), *run*, *rerun*, *camera* column (camcol) and *field*) from the Catalog Archive System (CAS) in order to map from a coordinate of a location in the sky to a DR1 observation. The tables *Spectral Object*, *Spectral Best Target Selection Object* and *Spectral Target Selection Object* each have these attributes. While the CAS structure does not have any relations between tables, a derived relation between *Best Resource Description Framework Table* (bestrdf) and the *Best Target Selection Field* table by the *field* identification (fieldId) attribute shown in Chapter 5 is also a valid identification for any observation. In addition to these attributes, these tables contain attributes obtained from analysis of spectrographic and the photometric observation sources. In order to provide observation and analysis source file look up, there are some attributes that must be derived from the six key attributes. Photographic observations are recorded in five shades of color (green, indigo, red, ultra-violet, and Z). Let the base URL of where DR1 stores its photographic observations, x_0, be defined as follows:

$$x_0 = x_1/x_2/x_3$$

Equation 1 Photographic Observation Format

where x_1 is the base URL, x_2 is the run number, and x_3 is the rerun number. Also, the slashes are interpreted as literal characters. Each observation is stored in a directory called *coor*. Let the URL of a photographic observation, PhO_{URL}, be a defined as follows:

$$PhO_{\{URL\}} = x_2/x_3/coor/x_4/fpC - x_2 - c - x_4 - x_3 - x_5\{.fits.gz\}$$

Equation 2 Photographic URL

where x_2 and x_3 are as defined in Equation 1, x_4 is the camera column, x_5 is the field number, and c is the color. Also, the hyphens, and are interpreted as literal characters. The corrected images were further pre-processed into color images stored in JPEG format. The JPEG images are adequate for easy-to-retrieve prepared previews, but lack substantial amounts of pixel depth resolution thereby rendering them ineffective for deep scientific analysis. Each pre-computed JPEGs is stored in a directory called zoom with a sub-directory structure for camera column. Let the URL for a pre-computed JPEG image, x_6, be defined as follows:

$$x_6 = x_0/\text{zoom}/x_4/\text{fpC} - x_2 - x_4 - x_3 - x_5 - z - z_0 -.\text{jpeg}$$

Equation 3 Precomputed JPEG URL Formula

where x_0 is as defined in Equation 1; x_2, x_3, x_4 and x_5 are as defined in Equation 2; and z_0 is the zoom level number. Thus their URL is a derived attribute. The six key attributes can also be used to acquire the results of analytical pipelines.

Most tables in DR1 are oriented toward the observed object and not the observation. Therefore, many observed objects exist in the table for one observation. One way to render a single observation, a Spectral Object Comparator can reduce the collection of observed observations to the number observations referenced.

Section 2 Bridging Relational Databases to Object-Oriented Models

The Object Relational Machine (ORM) is a key mechanism for persistent documents and solves object consistency and concurrency problems in large scale metadata catalogs. This section examines the general structure of an ORM Engine and principles on which it was constructed. This examination is followed by a description of a general data flow scenario for such an engine. Lastly, it is shown how this structure can be extended for applications. It is this extension that is critical for web applications to provide the data and caching mechanisms. The rule-based system explored in this work regulates the caching and data flow features provided by the ORM.

Every ORM consists of a data model description group and an engine. The data model description group consists of a collection of description files and dictionaries that provide class constructing templates for producing *entity* classes. Each description file or dictionary typically maps one-to-one with a relational database instance. Any one row of a database table is mapped to a *m*anaged object, m_o. When a managed object is mapped from an enterprise database it is typically called an *e*nterprise object.

Data models descriptions are defined in terms of *d*ata models, entities, attributes and *r*elationships. A *data model* is a specification that maps a database schema into *entities*. An *entity* maps a row of a table into an Object-Oriented (OO) class. The *attributes* of a database are mapped into members of an *entity* called *attributes members*, and database relationships map into lookup methods called *relationships*. The collection and interaction between these objects form the basis of the Model-Entity-Relational-Attribute design pattern, which provides a layer of separation in an ORM design. This pattern is further augmented by another feature known as Key Value Coding (KVC) compliance described in (Buck and Yacktman 2010).

The ORM engine itself typically consists of the following layers: an editing context, an object store coordinator, an object store, and an adaptor layer. These layers work together to fulfill an internally consistent view constraint, as reported in (Hill and Anglin 2004). The internal consistent view constraint is defined as a state where the following holds:

- each m_o only has references to other m_o within the same editing context,

- any subset of managed objects $\overline{m_o}$ has a consistent graph mapping regardless of a start point,

- If an m_o is not presently in an editing context, E, then it is brought into E when referenced,

- and changes to m_o are reflected throughout the engine's layers.

Thus, we can define an ORM engine structure in this manner. Let the editing context E be defined as a set

$$E = \{c_i, \overline{m_o}\}$$

Equation 4: Editing Context

where c_i is a many-to-one reference to the *object store coordinator* (C) that references the instance of E, and $\overline{m_o}$ is a collection of managed objects. Let C be defined as follows:

$$C = \{\overline{s_1}, \overline{e}\}$$

where $\overline{s_1}$ is the collection of references to abstract database object contexts, $\overline{e}$ is a collection of references to editing contexts as defined in Equation 4: Editing Context. The run-time of object oriented languages such as Objective-C and Java provide a facade that makes the reference look like it is an instance of the object. In reality each object is individually contained and simply referenced by related objects. Also, note that the abstract database acts as a generic database to provide a facade of any supported databases. This provides the capability of supporting multiple RDBMS vendors while making the ORM model generic.

Let an abstract database object store, S, be defined as follows:

$$S = \{c, s_1, s_2, s_3, a_1, a_2, a_3\}$$

where s_1, s_2 and s_3 are references to a database context object, database store object, and database channel object, respectively. Similarly, a_1, a_2 and a_3 are references to adaptor context, adaptor store, and adaptor channel, respectively. The instance of object store coordinator referenced by the database context object coordinates the efforts of the objects in S to ensure that each set of m_o is a proper subset of database rows necessary to satisfy the consistent view constraint. The database store object analyzes changes made to each m_o in each editing context instance managed by the object store coordinator. The database store object hands off this list of changes to the managed objects to adaptor store through adapter channel. Database channel objects communicate with paired instances of adapter channels. This pairing allows a multi-threaded ORM the ability to manage many channels with many adaptor contexts. The adapter channel checks with the adapter context in order to transmit and receive data sources from the database adaptor. The adapter context maintains the adaptor's context, which ensures smooth transitioning states.

An ORM provides a mapping between database operations and the following actions:

- insert

- update

- delete

- retrieve

- query

- save

- revert

- undo

- redo

The first four satisfy the notion of the Create Read Update and Design (CRUD) architecture as shown in (Thomas 2003). The query is typically implemented as a form of Domain Relational Calculus described by (Kifer, Bernstein et al. 2006). The save, revert, undo, and redo operations fit a managed pattern. Each of these actions have transition operations for conditions of will, did and have done the action.

Each member of facade group maintains state on each action, and determines how to fulfill the desired effect. There is one other state that is not included in this action list. A fault state exists if a pair of m_o, say a and b, satisfies the following conditions:

- a is related to b

- b is loaded into E

- a is not loaded, but a place holder exists because b is loaded.

- a is requested because of b.

Managing fault states is a classic problem, and ORMs manage this state to balance database traffic cost issues. These issues can be managed, and tools are typically supplied to do so. However, there is not a known solution that applies to all possible distinct instances of this problem. Enterprise Objects supplies two fault handling memory caching systems: the default and Batch Display Group. This issue is examined more thoroughly in Chapter 5 .

The bridging pattern has a powerful implementation as a consequence of using a mature ORM. Only the model and business logic were necessary to be specified to provide the facade of an observational model. Furthermore, this bridge provides a mechanism to fulfill the Model View Controller paradigm used to define RIQS in each form created.

Section 3 Building Web Responses with Models and Actions

An *action application oriented* builder uses two invocations on the basis of state to access the whole web application, called *c*omponent actions and *d*irect actions. Furthermore, the web application itself should be represented by a class that manages the entry point, thread control, network abstractions for handling HTTP requests, and calling on actions to generate responses here called the *t*he application class. A component action inherently uses a server-side state that is maintained by a session object. All component action URLs are dynamically generated to include references to the component that generated them, the sessions the component belongs to, and the context in which they were constructed. Direct actions are inherently stateless and invoked by static URLs. Direct actions can invoke components the same as component actions. Both sets of actions are handled by sub-classes of an action request handler to produce special response types such web services, grid services, or remote procedure call handlers. The concept of MVC component driven applications provide a facility to enforce the design patterns of a content management system.

Section 4 Revised Image Query Service (RIQS)

Enterprise Objects (EO) contribute to reassembling data acquired from the DR1 (Data Release) collection. DR1 contains meta-data used to identify photographic objects needed for spectrographic observations (Raddick, The SDSS collaboration 2003). The attributes contained in the meta-data include *N*ear Field (NF) Calibration, astrometric calibration, correlated image references, and other data calibration processes . The calibration data is a collection of metrics necessary to align the photographic observations and supply correct astrometric reference which includes the observed object's standard coordinate data. The standard coordinate reference metric is crucial for identifying both the objects in the meta-data, and determining the coordinates of the objects in photographic observations. Both the observation designation attributes and astrometric meta-data are contained in the DR1 database as tables referred to as *S*pectral Object and *S*pectral Object Target (Stoughton 2006) . The primary relationship in the DR1 schema for RIQS is the Spectral Object (SO) table.

An EO model can be used to define and construct a database table. There are open source tools for producing an EO model from an existing database. The EO model for RIQS was reverse engineered from the DR1 (Data Release 1) database and appropriate Java data-types were assigned to map the attributes as illustrated in Figure 2. The WebObjects Framework supplies a Java class called *E*O Generic Record that provides a facade to represent each EO entity as a KVC compliant Java class ((Mendis 2002, Hill and Anglin 2004)). If there are no derived attributes, the *E*O Generic Record provides all the necessary bindings to connect elements in the view specification to attributes in the EO model.

If there is an entity where derived attributes or other customization is required, then there are tools to generate sub-classes of the generic record specifically for a particular EO entity. The generated class is named the SO class.

The members of this Java class are the EO attributes which are also shown in Figure 2. The derived attributes for a given EO entity are contained in a SO subclass. The SO subclass defines a *b*usiness logic class that provides the URLs for each pre-computed JPEG image and original photographic observation in a FITS format such as shown in Figure 1. The technique of sub-classing a generated generic record of an entity to include such business logic is referred to as the Generational Gap Pattern ((Hill and Anglin 2004)).

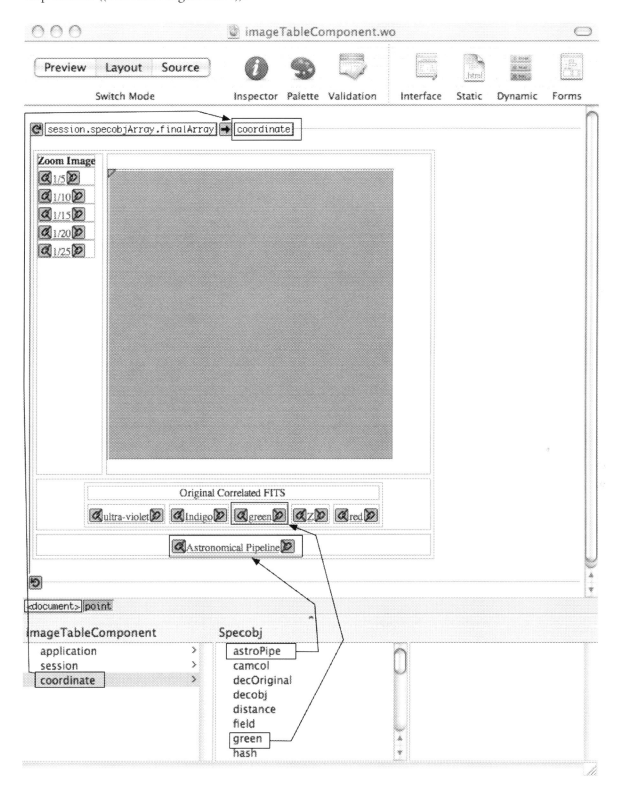

Figure 1 Photographic Observation Image Table Component

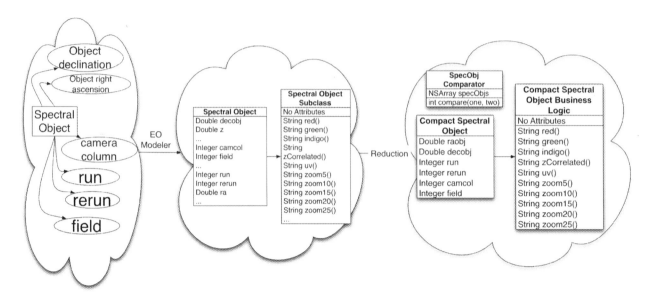

Figure 2 EO Modeler Transformation

The Spectral Object table shown in Figure 2 lists many meta-data attributes for both the spectral analysis and image processing of each astronomical object recorded. Since most of these attributes are not necessary for image retrieval, the EO model generated can be streamlined from an over-specified model shown in Figure 2 in the middle compared with a reduced Spectral Object entity on the right. If the application is restricted to solely retrieving images, the Spectral Object table is then limited to six attributes as they are the only attributes required to identify a specific astronomical object, plus a hidden key attribute contained in the table, i.e., the object id. This reduction results in an entity much smaller than the whole Spectral Object original entity; the new object entity will be referred to as a *Compact Spectral Object* entity. Each Compact Spectral Object is contained in the Compact Spectral Object Model Array, which is analogous to the Compact Spectral Object table. Also shown in Figure 2 is an object called the Compact Spectral Object Comparator, which sorts the Compact Spectral Model Array.

The revised IQS widget (observation box) is not required to identify each object in the entire region requested but only the observation itself. Each observation may contain hundreds of different objects recorded in the Compact Spectral Object table. Thus, the revised IQS includes a support class called *Duplicate Observation Eliminator*, shown in Figure 2, that eliminates repeated observations which are generated by each object associated with the observation.

Section 5 Revised Image Query Service (RIQS) Illustration

Figure 3 shows the position query form for the user to enter right ascension (*a*) and declination (δ) coordinates as parameters to query for observations. The default region when RIQS is loaded is the celestial prime meridian at the equator. If the user wants one of the observations near these selected coordinates, all is needed is to scroll down and visually spot the observation patch desired.

Once the observation desired is found, the *r*epeating observation (image) boxes gives the user access to the data archive files. The zoom links, shown on the left side, supply pre-computed JPEG images in a separate browser. The observation image shown is a $\frac{1}{15}$ scale image.

The user also has the option of selecting the original FITS images. SDSS (Sloan Digital Sky Survey) acquired these observations using five different filters and therefore produced five different source images. This revision of IQS supports a browser's default behavior by providing the link to the FITS file. If the browser has a FITS viewer, the FITS file will be viewed in a new browser window. If the browser does not provide a viewer, the default behavior is to download the FITS file to the user's disk. Both sets of links supply the user the ability to retrieve the content.

The query form provides the means to query the organization of the image database. The RIQS interface does not restrict the range of values the user may enter for astronomical coordinates. α values range from (–24,24), and δ from (–180,180). As described in Building Web Responses with Models and Actions and Revised Image Query Service (RIQS) a set of observations for any point in the sky requested is returned. So the user supplies the coordinates in the form shown in Figure 3.

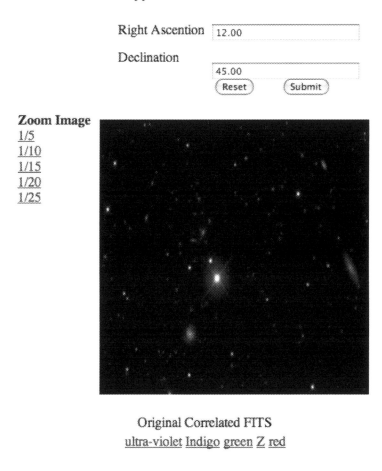

Figure 3 User selected section of the sky with selection form and one observation.

RIQS is open source and to run only requires a WO web adapter, which is also open source. The original DR1 (Data Release 1) IQS requires many customized tools and therefore with limited distribution for image processing on pre-computed JPEG images. Because RIQS reduces image retrieval to one web application minimizes the probability of failure of the image retrieval process due to changes introduced on the tools otherwise used.

It accomplishes a namespace control by the simplification of its interface. RIQS has a limited control over its namespace although it can be further simplified, it still provides an easy method for devising such control and also supplies a separate web service. Thus, third party web applications can override the behavior of these boxes to suit their needs. Amongst the tagged items are the links for each of the FITS files references, which is something that neither DR1 nor DR6 provides.

CHAPTER 4

A MOBILE CODE ARCHITECTURE

Section 1 Data Models For A Generic Photographic Observation Catalog

The model described in this section is another Object Relational Mapper (ORM) description that facilitates expansion by allowing entities such as photographic observations to be generalized so as to represent a broader set of objects. This is accomplished by a reduction of attributes to a set common to all astronomical observations $\mathcal{O}$, such that:

$$\mathcal{O} = \{d, s, v\}$$

Equation 5 Observation Model

where d is the *date*, s is the *site*, and v is the *version*.

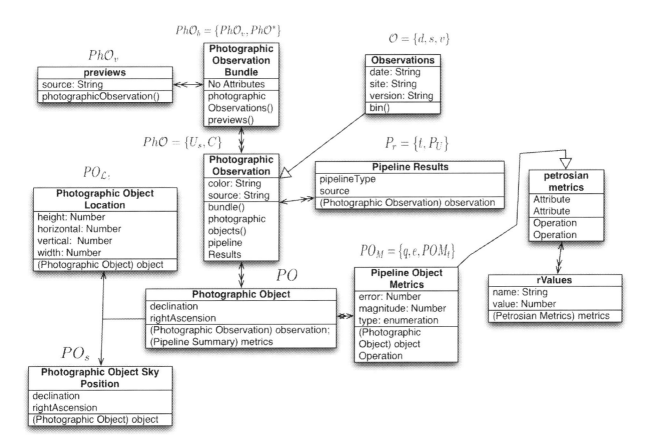

Figure 4 Observation Class Stucture

Each photographic or optical observation is obtained by a procedure called *scanning*. An optical observation includes many areas at the same time or in the same area with different color filters. A color optical scan is a procedure that focuses a telescope at a particular portion of the night sky and supplies different color filters to produce many images characterized by different wavelengths. Color scans are typically a physical procedure accomplished at the interface between the CCD and the telescope's focal point. A strip optical scan advances the telescope to obtain a collage image of CCD width. These are typically accomplished at the focal point by moving the CCD about the focal point, but it can also be accomplished by moving the telescope itself in a precise pattern. In both forms of strip scanning, the images are assembled by a form of image registration ((Kitchin 2003)).

The color photographic observation, PO, is defined as a tuple:

$$PO = \{U_s, C\}$$

Equation 6 Photographic Observation Model

where U_s is the *s*ource URL and C is the color of the observation's filter as shown in the iFITS data model in Figure 4. Such an observation may relate to calibration analysis results, and many observed objects. Each strip of observations is referenced by a set of Observed Pair O_p and Observation Segments O_s. The attributes for the observed pair and segments are derived from DR1's Best Target Source Segment table. Each strip also has a derived property of groups of observations that were color scanned together, and this entity is called the photographic observation bundle (*PB*) represented as follows:

$$PB = \{Pr, PO^*\}$$

Equation 7 Photographic Observation Bundle Model

as shown in the top left section in Figure 4.. *Pr* is an array of previews and PO^* refers to the collection of POs in Equation 6.

SDSS uniquely categorizes each scan of the same area with different color filters by the critical attributes *r*un, *r*erun, *c*amera column, and *f*ield. The color scan set for each bundle *PB* is acquired within minutes of each other thereby deriving a consolidated single color image that is represented as the preview entity, *Pr*. A bundle *PB* can have many previews based on resolution and size such as the pre-computed JPEGs in DR1.

For each photographic observation there is a set of pipeline results. These results were stored in FITS files in DR1, but this may not always be the case. Each one of these calibration are well-known operations that are included in standard tools. Let *C* denote the calibration analysis record described as follows:

$$C = \{t, u\}$$

Equation 8 Pipeline Result Model

where t is the attribute calibration type and u is the URL source of the calibration record. This is also shown in Figure 4. The URL source can be either a FITS file or a specification to produce a particular result by a set of affiliated tools.

The tables in DR1 such as the Spectral Object table, Target Source Fields, and multiple Target Source Object tables all contain selected metrics obtained from each of the calibrations. Each one of these metrics belong to individual photographic source objects (or articles) PA shown in Figure 4. Photographic sources are detected in each observation and derived by individual tests in the calibrations. Each of the attributes of the Target Source Fields and Object tables can be considered from a generic point of view. Let DR represent a single data reduction metric and define it as:

$$DR = \{q \ e \ t\}$$

Equation 9 Pipeline Object Metrics

where q is the metric value, e is the error, and t is the type of DR recorded. Sub-classes of DR exist to handle special cases of metrics such as Petrosian analysis.

The observed object can be defined as its own entity. Each source article, A, has a relation to each observed position. Every article in the night sky is identified by its common name and its location relative to previously known references. Each PS has a relation to its observed position in the sky SL and optical image observation IL. It is also related to an entity representing the A that has a common name or designation attribute.

Section 2 Mapping Observed Objects back to Observations

The combined set of SO table attributes can be divided into two sub-domains: the critical attributes and the selected metrics. DR1 is based on mapping ((The SDSS collaboration 2003)) the critical attribute tuples to the URL references. The summary metric domain consists of attributes that correspond to metrics gleaned from the analysis results, optical observations themselves, and in some cases observations from spectrographic instruments. Examples of such metrics include the object's location in the sky, its location in the image/observation, values acquired by Petrosian analysis, and Point Spread Function coefficients, etc. A mapping procedure of these attributes is necessary to allow a complete use of the SO table.

A dictionary, p_d, is composed of key-value pairs that are defined as follows:

$$p_d = \{k, v\}$$

Equation 10 Dictionary Structure

where k is a string that represents the element key, and v is the value of the element and can be any data-type. Let each row of the SO table is be represented by a dictionary denoted SO_D. Likewise, each table-entity in the iFITS data model can also be represented in dictionary form. In particular let $\hat{PB}$ denote PB as described in Equation 7 in dictionary form and let $\hat{PA}$ denote PA. A mapping mechanism is needed to determine $\hat{PB}$ and $\hat{PA}$. To implement the mapping mechanism generating $\hat{PB}$ let f_1 denote a mapping function such that

$$f_1: \{SO_D, URL_o\} \rightarrow \hat{PB}$$

Equation 11 Bundle Function.

where URL_o is the URL of the DR1 repository that provided SO_D. f_1 creates each of the members of $\hat{PB}$ from four of the critical attributes in the SO table, *run*, *rerun*, camera column (*camcol*) and *field*. Each $\hat{PB}$ consists of three P_d tuples (as described in Equation 8) defined as follows:

$$\hat{PB} = \{\{k_1, x_1\}, \{k_2, x_2\}, \{k_3, x_3\}\}$$

Equation 12 : Dictionary Photographic Observation Bundle

where k_i is the key in the corresponding tuple, $i=1,2,3$. Likewise x_i are the values for the corresponding tuples, $i=1,2,3$. The generated string value x_1 is uniquely constructed from the four critical attributes, denoted PB_k, that serve as the PB identity string. The value x_2 is an array containing photographic observation preview dictionaries $\hat{Pr}$ that correspond to the Pr entity described in Section 1. The value x_3 is an array containing photographic observation dictionaries $\hat{PO}[c]$ that correspond to PO described in Equation 6 such that

$$\hat{PO}[c] = \{\{k_4, c\}, \{k_5, x_5\}, \{k_6, x_6\}\{k_7, x_7\}\}$$

Equation 13 Photographic Observation Dictionaries

where the k_i and x_i are as described in Equation 1. The URL as described in Equation 4 U_s is represented by x_5; x_6 corresponds to an array of pipeline results in dictionary form while x_7 corresponds to an array of $\hat{PA}$, which is an exception for Equation 9. The f_1 in Equation 11 does not compute out the members of x_7; rather it simply allocates the array.

The design choice is justified by the relation differences between PB at large and PA. There is a one to many relationship between PB and SO, and this relationship is determined by PB_k. Therefore, any implementation of the mapping mechanism should test if PB_k is in the array of $\hat{PB}$ or not. If it is, then f_1 in Equation 9 has already been determined for a previous SO_D and does not need to be determined again. Otherwise, f_1 must be computed.

In either case, for any SO_D there is a $\hat{PB}$ determined by lookup or by Equation 9. The relationship for PA to SO, on the other hand, is one to one, and therefore requires a second function to populate x_7 in Equation 11, in other words, a mapping mechanism such that

$$f_2: SO_D \rightarrow \hat{PA}$$

The mapping of *PA* in Chapter 4 Section 1 to $\hat{PA}$ causes *PA*'s relations to *IL*, *SL*, and *A* to also be mapped into equivalent dictionaries. Also the mapping of *PA* causes *DR* to be mapped into an equivalent array of dictionaries $\hat{DB}$.

Section 3 Marshaling a Catalog Archive Service

Sub-Section 1 Marshaling

The implementation of the iFITS mapping requires a transmission of the Spectral Object (SO) table. The resulting mashup code improves the performance of RIQS as long as the flow of data is optimized while satisfying queries that may need to consume any subset of the SO table. As previously stated in section, RIQS represents *SO* as an array of dictionaries (SO_D). Therefore, marshaling *SO* is a mapping function *M* defined as follows

$$M: SO_D \rightarrow \overline{SO_D}$$

Equation 14 HTML Mapping function

where $\overline{SO_D}$ is the marshaled form of SO_D. The marshaling function is a bijection, i.e., all forms of Equation 6 include some type of language transformation from one representation to another. For example, DR6 and RIQS both have a HTML template that allows them to render the marshaled form of SO_D as a web page. DR6's IQS communicates in tabular form the attributes in the top row. Also, it includes the values of the subset of *SO*, which are requested in the subsequent rows. RIQS includes in its HTML production an automated construction of links to each source and pipeline result pertaining to each SO_D that presents those results in HTML form. RIQS has another marshaling method included by its web services, called eXtensible Markup Language (XML) Property Lists (plists) that was introduced by NeXT as described in (Hillegaus 2004, Butler 2005, Anderson 2008). XML plists use a two-step marshaling method such that

$$M_1: \{M_2: SO \rightarrow p_{SO}\} \rightarrow x_{SO}$$

where p_{SO} is the SO in a plist structure; M_2 is a function from SO tables to a SO plist; M_1 is a mapping function from a plist to XML document, and x_{SO} is SO XML plist. NeXT's plist includes five fundamental data-types *s*tring, number, date, boolean, and *r*aw data and two compound types *a*rrays and *d*ictionaries. Dictionaries are as described in Equation 8, and both arrays and dictionaries can hold values of any plist type. x_{SO} is the XML form of p_{SO}. RIQS's web service inherits XML plists from the WebObjects frameworks with web services shown in (Feiler 2002, Hill and Anglin 2004, Beatty and Lopez-Benitez 2009).

Sub-Section 2 Overhead Analysis

DR6 IQS and RIQS's web service each have their respective overhead. In this section, we highlight the overhead cost of the HTML marshaling function used by DR6's IQS, and the XML plists used by RIQS's web services.

In order for a HTML table structure to be a viable marshaling structure, its scheme must be arranged to prevent breaking the un-marshaling parser or must utilize the Document Object Model (DOM) tree structure of the HTML table. Such a scheme includes a header and foot that impose a fifteen character overhead. Each row and column impose another beginning and ending tag that carry a nine character overhead. If DR6's IQS only supplies seven critical attributes (run, rerun, camera column, field, α, δ, and object ID), then there is a eighty-one character overhead per row.

XML-plist's schema includes tags for each data-type that are labeled dictionary, array, string, number, data, boolean, and date. Therefore, each dictionary carries an overhead of thirteen characters for the beginning and the end. Each element of the dictionary has eleven characters for the key, plus the overhead for its values. Every array carries a fifteen character overhead for the beginning and end, plus the overhead for each of its members. The fundamental data types carry an overhead of seventeen for string and number, thirteen for data and date, and nineteen for boolean types. Thus, for each row of SO, XML plist carries an overhead of 209 characters. Therefore, it is more costly than the HTML. Even though it is better defined and usable by web service clients.

Sub-Section 3 An Improved Marshaling Structure

A technique is proposed that is a hybrid of XML plists and a marshaling language based on the JavaScript language known as JavaScript Object Notation. The resulting plists are referred to as JSON Property lists (JSON-plists), and can be included in either the web applications or a web service similar to LEWOStuff's JSON-RPC as described in (Lindesay 2008).

In order to describe JSON-plists, we use the Backus-Naur Form (BNF) notation such as used in (Cooke 2003). Such a form represents the language in terms of production rules, terminal symbols and non-terminal symbols.

Dictionaries are defined by a JavaScript structure called objects. The values accepted by these objects include string, number, date, boolean, arrays and objects. The production rule for a JavaScript object is as follows:

$$O_d \leftarrow \{O_d{}'\}$$

Equation 15 JSON Object

where O_d is the non-terminal symbol representing a whole JavaScript object, the braces are terminal symbols, and $O_d{}'$ is a non-terminal symbol representing key-value pairs of the object. This production rule allows the parsing of a set of JavaScript symbols and determines that they are an object. Likewise, $O_d{}'$ is defined such that

$$O_d{}' \leftarrow k : V_j O_d{}''$$

Equation 16 JSON Object Element

where k is defined as in Equation 8, V_j is a non-terminal symbol representing the values of the dictionary, and $O_d{}''$ is a non-terminal symbol allowing $O_d{}'$ to be parsed for every key-value pair in the object. Lastly, the production rule for V_j is nearly the same as in XML plists such that:

$$V_j \leftarrow \mathcal{V}|true|false$$

Equation 17 JSON Value True or False

where $\mathcal{V}$ is a terminal symbol representing the marshaled form of a string, number or date; and and are terminating symbols for boolean values. Thus, the $\mathcal{V}$ represents the same overhead as the other two methods by definition.

Therefore, the overhead for a JSON-plist dictionary is two characters for the beginning and end plus the size of the keys. For the SO_D, the cost of JSON-plist per row is twenty-five characters. This is nearly a 4 to 13 ratio between the JSON-plist and the HTML table used by DR6's IQS. Furthermore, the array representing the SO table carries only two characters overhead, as opposed to the thirteen for either XML-plist or HTML tables.

Section 4 Building a Mobile Agent

The last feature of RIQS to migrate is the user interface representation. RIQS utilizes a compound design pattern called the Model-View-Controller (MVC) ({Buck, 2010 #891;Gamma, 1994 #908;Gamma, 1993 #672}). The RIQS user interface incorporates MVC as a 3-tuple; composed of a controller containing outlets and actions ({Hill, 2004 #867;Mendis, 2002 #983}), a view that is defined by a Web Object Description (WOD), and a data model ((Feiler 2002, Beatty and Lopez-Benitez 2009)). The controller binds both the view and model together to form the MVC 3-tuple component.

An *o*utlet is a passive member of the controller that contains data to be consumed by the view. An *a*ction is a method of the controller that is bound to some member of the view such as a button, hyperlink, etc. A WOD consists of a web page and a binding specification, which connects each outlet and action to the elements of the web page. In this case, the web page specifies the appearance of the component and constitutes the view specification.

A view can contain references to many other components and allows the construction of elaborate displays. Each view specification is loaded by the controller upon initialization and is followed by the binding operation. The concept of a view specification can be incorporated into the iFITS mashup to provide similar functionality.

Mashups exist and interact in a browser's DOM (Document Object Model), which represents a web page and all its contents. The DOM is inherently represented as a tree structure based on the production rules for HTML[10]. The header, footer, and body of the web page form the first triplet leaves. Subsequent elements are represented as additional leaves. Mashups use JavaScript's DOM libraries to add and remove elements from the web-page that the JavaScript is written on.

The mashup's MVC is analogous to the MVC used in RIQS, but its supporting libraries are more rudimentary in order to make it more mobile. As in RIQS, the controller object must perform needed bindings. Once the bindings are performed, the controller can then attach the MVC component to the tree. The view is specified by an HTML source generated by RIQS and performs the following two view specification functions:

---

[10] WWW Consortium http://www.w3.org/TR/html401/

1. The mashup component controller constructs a view specification for itself,
2. The mashup loads its data model from the web page supplied by RIQS.

The views thus constructed are useful to migrate image previews, which are referred to as repeating observation boxes in (Beatty and Lopez-Benitez 2009). A graphical floating container system is proposed to represent observations, analysis, and pre-computed images. A *c*ontainer is a component object that provides a common set of interface actions and outlets, a reference to its environment interface, and a generic component ((Anderson and Anderson 1998)){Dewsbury, 2007 #923}. A *g*adget is a component object tuple that supplies a common interface to its container ({Dewsbury, 2007 #922}) and defines a graphical *l*ayout ((Fogarty and Hudson 2003)) for a specific purpose. Each floating-container possesses a gadget of some kind as its generic component.

Like RIQS, the iFITS mashup includes a gadget to represent each image preview of a color photographic observation. Each gadget is instantiated from an array containing information about the preview. Each gadget contains references for additional information about that observation. Unlike RIQS, the color photographic observation bundle gadget can reference other gadgets that represent each entity of the iFITS data model. Also unlike RIQS, the user can manipulate, reduce, or close floating containers.

The creation of gadgets follows the model proposed in {Gamma, 1994 #908}. As shown in Figure 5, an abstract factory constructs a group of objects of similar purpose by using a matching set of factories. The common object to be constructed is the *i*FITS gadget that serves as a template to represent each entity-object in the iFITS data model. The most prominent sub-class of the iFITS gadget is the FITS Preview Gadget.

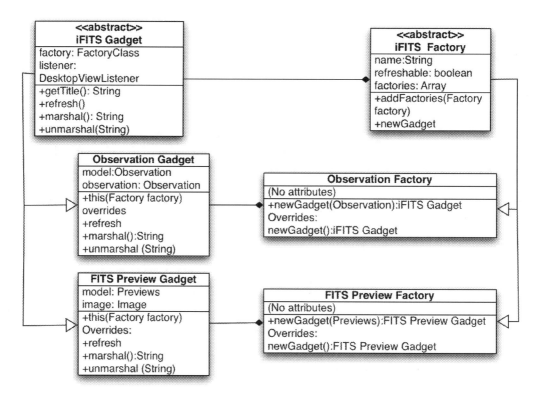

Figure 5 Gadget Object UML

Abstract containers use creator classes called factories to generate product classes as illustrated in Figure 5. Each factory can create a gadget, and the specific factory sub-class determines which container subclass to create. The factory contains a list of subclasses for each type of gadget available and provides the structure for initiating new containers.

Upon loading the web page instance containing the iFITS mashup, the following initial steps are performed:

1. Load the JSON-plist from its web-page instance, and marshal it into a Spectral Object (SO) table,
2. Load the iFITS data model,
3. Once loaded, the mashup binds each photographic observation in the iFITS data model to a preview gadget, and
4. Finally, the mashup displays them.

This process leaves RIQS query components intact. Therefore, any query through RIQS is processed as before, and the query process becomes transparent to the user. Even with the overhead of loading the iFITS mashup code, the iFITS interface shown in Figure 6 is expected to gain a speedup of three due to the reduced overhead in the mashup's JSON-plist marshaling.

Figure 6 Fire Mashup Default

CHAPTER 5

RULE-BASED CONTEXT MANAGEMENT ARCHITECTURE

DR1 separated its query services based on observation type. There was an image query service, and there was a spectral query service. Each query service had a series of services to render reports. These reports were augmented with instructions on how to obtain the related observations and calibration output files. For example, spatial queries could allow for photographic images to be combined.

Instead of trying to reproduce two separate query services, this chapter introduces a different approach. It also explores the notion of a catalog based on natural expansion of generic structures. Like challenges observed in (Berriman 2011), this work addresses the massive archive issues of astronomy. In order to implement this scheme, this chapter examines an emerging technology. Many indie enterprises have emerged and flourished as a consequence of this emerging technologies properties for rapid development, deployment, and elegant refinement.

This work does not attempt to restructure the data as suggested in (Beatty and Lopez-Benitez 2010) or accommodate cloud computing architectures. Although, the emerging technology does contribute an architecture related to cloud computing, namely Web 2.0 as described in . (Shuen 2008, Raivio 2009) Lastly, this chapter shows an illustration of this query service demonstrating the mapping scheme. The work presented in this chapter constitutes has been submitted as (Beatty and Lopez-Benitez 2011). This work examines issues such as size and capacity which are crucial when considering cloud computing as an alternative architecture. Work in Chapter 6 further expands on the work in this chapter to offer the capability of migrating to cloud assets, allowing data owners to reduce the costs and risks associated with maintaining large data collections.

Section 1 Obtaining Access To The Observation Sources

DR1 has both spectroscopic and photographic observation types. Both of these types were stored as image FITS files. Also, DR1 includes are analysis results files. The results are stored as FITS tables or binary files. DR1's web interface shared these observations and analysis using the following services: a foot service, an image query service, and spectral query service. The image and spectral query services allows queries on properties of the observation. Some of these properties were obtained through analysis of the images (spectral or photographic) themselves. These services never included the entire set of attributes of the Catalog Archive Service. Such a set of pages were deemed to immense to construct.

From the query results, a user would receive a series of attributes values. These values would be plugged into the Data Archive Service. This service would determine what files were relevant for the series attributes provided. The user would then copy and paste a set of instructions into a terminal where the Data Archive Service (DAS) would copy the associated files to the user's hard disk.

This section provides a description of the sources and the attributes used to define their naming scheme. These descriptions serve as a basis to add a business logic that automates the DAS procedure.

First, let some terms be clarified. According to (Stoughton and et.al. 2002) a data stream from a single CCD in a *scanline* is cut into a series of *frames* (mono-wavelength images of the size of one CCD). Likewise, "a *scanline* is data from a single set of CCDs that sweep the same area of the sky," page 1581 of (York 2000). The photographic CCD for SDSS has six columns, each with a separate wavelength filter. The area swept by this CCD is called a *strip*. A *frame* in five filters for the same part of the sky are called a *field*. Lastly a *run* is a set of data collected from a continuous pass of the sky with the same telescope.

Sub-Section 1 The File Structure Established in the Early Data Release of the Sloan Digital Sky Survey

The first type of data files contained in the Data Archives of DR1 is the *object photographic output*. An *object photographic output* is a list of metrics produced by the *frames* calibration. The name scheme consists of the attributes *run*, *field number*, and *camera column*. These attributes are arranged in the following format:

```
imaging/$run/$rerun/objcs
/$camcol/fpObjc-{$run}-{$camcol}-{$field}.fit
```

There are also 4 by 4 binned versions of each the corrected images after a *sky* subtraction calibration. This particular image is a result of the frames calibration. Each of these files can be located by the following format:

```
imaging/$run/$rerun/objcs
/$camcol/fpBIN-{$run}-{$filter}{$camcol}-{$field}.fit
```

The atlas images serve the purpose of determining approximate distances of sources from Earth. These values can be useful in finding what are referred to as *Origin of E+A galaxies* in (Bekki, Couch et al. 2005, Goto 2005) . The URL for these files have the following pattern.

```
imaging/$run/$rerun/objcs/$camcol/
fpAtlas-{$run}-{$camcol}-{$field}.fit
```

Another FITS file is the *fields statistics table*. It contains a statistical summary of the results of the *frame* window calibration (*framew*) described in (Stoughton and et.al. 2002) for one field. Many of these statistics were later recorded in the Spectral Object and Fields tables. The location format for this file is as follows:

```
imaging/$run/$rerun/objcs/$camcol/
fpFieldStat-{$run}-{$camcol}-{$field}.fit
```

Each *frame* has a mask. The *frames* calibration applies these masks as an input. Those masks were stored by the following pattern.

```
imaging/$run/$rerun/objcs
/$camcol/fpM-{$run}-{$filter}{$camcol}-{$field}.fit
```

There is another photographic calibration that takes *fields* tables and a set of PSF fitted metadata generated by the frames calibration as inputs. This analysis is called a *preliminary photometric calibration*. These calibrations are described in (Heasley 1999), and these tables may be found by the following format.

```
imaging/$run/$rerun/objcs/$camcol/
psField-{$run}-{$filter}{$camcol}-{$field}.fit
```

The *astrometric calibration* produces a set of *astrometric transformations* for every field in an imaging run. *Astrometric calibration* is a form of image registration to match up image pixel coordinates in the frame to sky coordinates (in this case great circle coordinates) using a standard collection of known sources. Much of this registration involves comparing each of the color observation images against each other. The coordinates of the great circle are described in terms of two axes: μ and ν for longitude and lattitude respectively. Each *astrometric transformation* is stored in the DAS repository. The location of these transformations is defined in terms of *run*, *rerun*, and *camera column* using the following pattern.

```
imaging/$run/$rerun/astrom/asTrans-{$run}.fit
```

The *Final Photometric Calibration* is produced by matching photographic frames to the monitor telescope's observations. The result of this calibration is called a *calibrated patch* in (Tucker and et.al. 2006). This calibration's purpose is to provide a step in registering the observed image by using an image from the monitor telescope taken of the same patch of sky at roughly the same time. The *calibrated patches* may be found using the following pattern.

```
imaging/$run/$rerun/nfcalib/fcPCalib-{$run}-{$camcol}.fit
```

Each set of corrected frames can be located in terms of *run*, *rerun*, *field number*, *camera column* and filter (color). As there are only six colors, these values can be assumed and therefore fetched according to the following pattern.

```
imaging/$run/$rerun/corr/$camcol
/psField-{$run}-{$filter}{$camcol}-{$field}.fit
```

The 1-D spectral image consists of line measurements and red-shift determinations for each astronomical object. These metrics were summed over all of the exposures taken by a mapped plate. These images can be found based on the Modified Julian Date (MJD), the identification of the *plate* used to position the spectroscope's fibers, and the particular *fiber* group used to record the spectrum of the astronomical object.

```
spectro/1d_20/$plate/spSpec-{$MJD}-{$plate}-{$frame}.fit
spectro/ss_20/$plate/spSpec/spSpec-{$mjd}-{$plate}-{$frame}.fit
```

The *Spectral Plate* file was produced by a utility named idlspec2d as shown in (Hyde and Bernardi 2008). The spectral observations has metrics for flux and wavelength calibrated spectra over every exposure for a given mapped plate. It also has metrics of the environmental conditions at the time and place where a spectroscopic observation was made. The source record of these metrics can be found by the following pattern.

```
spectro/2d_20/$plate/spPlate-{$plate}-{$mjd}.fit
```

There are atlas images for sources observed through spectroscopic plates in the DAS repository. For each spectroscopic observation, there are ten atlas images per file. Each atlas image corresponds to best and target photographic images for each shade. These images are arranged in terms of *plate*, *frame* and *MJD* in the following pattern.

```
spectro/ss_20/$plate/spAtlas/
spAtlas-{$plate}-{$mjd}-{$frame}.fit
```

There are notions of calibrated photographic and spectroscopic data for astronomical sources. Some of this data comes from reference diagnostics for 1-D spectroscopic observations. The diagnostic reference files are arranged in terms of plate and MJD in accordance with the following pattern.

```
spectro/ss_20/$plate/
spDiag1d-{$mjd}-{$plate}.par
```

The DR1 Spectral Object table also references the *P*late and Tile plug parameters defined by the following pattern:

```
spectro/ss_20/$plate/
plPlugMapM-{$plate}-{$mjd}-{$plateMap}{pointer}.par
```

where *plateMap* is an unique integer over the mapper run and *pointer* is an identifier which can be blank. Lastly, there are data stored in FITS binary tables called the *Spectroscopic Data for Objects* (sources) and the files are found using the following pattern.

```
spectro/ss_20/$plate/
spObj-{$plate}-{$mjd}-{$rerun}.fits
```

Sub-Section 2 Archive Access through Business Logic and Component Actions

Just as pertinent as what files are available in the data access catalog (DAS), a description of each table in DR1 provides a means to provide a mapping of file types to table type. This description includes seven table types. Some table types are described as a group since they have the same structure and differ only as to their purpose.

The classic approach taken by SDSS DR2 and other catalogs has been to confine the association of files to database tables by a means of business logic. The concept of business logic is a set of rules typically implemented in middleware with an object-oriented language to control the access and derivations of a data coming from an RDBMS. In the case of an ORM based system, this implementation is in the class associated with *entity* described in Chapter 3 Section 2 .

Target Selection Segment

One of the first tables constructed by SDSS was the target-segment (TS) tables. These tables were a record and plan for acquiring photographic observations. One of the attributes in the TS tables is chunk id. The remaining attributes serve as metrics measuring for each observation taken by the telescope. These metrics are *stripe number*, *strip*, and the four critical photographic attributes (*run, rerun, camera column* and *field*). SDSS divides the sky in to a series of overlapping stripes, each precisely 2.5 degrees wide. Each stripe consists of a pair of strips each containing six scanlines, 13 arcmin wide as described in (Gunn, Carr et al. 1998, York 2000, Gunn, Siegmund et al. 2006).There is a correspondence table that can be added to provide correspondence map between run and strip.

1. stripe number
2. strip
3. run
4. rerun
5. camcol
6. field0
7. number of fields

There is a second grouping of metrics in the target selection. These values apply to the observation segments of the sky. In essence, it was a check list for planned observations of parts of the sky. These metrics are as follows.

1. inclination
2. node
3. start mu
4. end mu
5. start mu deg
6. end mu deg
7. chunk id
8. chunk stripe
9. chunk start mu
10. chunk end mu
11. status

Since this table has the four critical attributes, business logic can add URL references of the photographic observations and analysis (used to construct *links*) to the TS segment report. These references include object photographic output, sky subtraction calibration, atlas, field statistics, frame calibration masks, preliminary photometric calibration, astrometric transformations, final photometric calibrations, and postage stamp fields. Business logic can not add a link containing a query to TS *fields*, but it can be a *direct action* as described in Chapter 3 Section 4 . This link is constructed by an ORM query on the TS fields table with a the shared attribute, *field*.

Target Selection Fields

The *target selection fields* (*TS Fields*) attributes come from the final calibrations of photographic observations shown in Section 1 . This applies to the basic four calibrations for CCD images shown in (Howell 2000): bias, zero, flat-field and noise. DR1 applied these calibrations to the two subsets of photographic observations: target and best. The attributes necessary to reference the spectral observations are not directly present in this table. This table does contain the four critical attributes for SDSS photographic observations. Therefore, these attributes justify the inclusion of the photographic observations and their calibrations through business logic. Just like *TS segments*, this work adds references through business logic and *direct action* actions. Query links are added via *direct actions* for *RDF* and *TS segment* tables. Thus the footprint service is replaced by the application of component action and business logic combination.

Z Emission and Cross Correlation

The Z channel of the photographic observations measures a sliver of the infrared section of the spectrum, which has a wavelength approximately $7.4 \cdot 10^{-10}$m. For redshift estimation there are choices of sources to measure. These source measurements are extracted from the indigo ($1.8 \cdot 10^{-10}$m) and red ($1.2 \cdot 10^{-10}$m) corrected frames as shown in (Stoughton and et.al. 2002). The Z tables (*Z Emission* and *Z Cross-Correlation*) have a *spectral object identifier* that can reference related sources from the spectral object (SO) table family. There are not sufficient attributes to link any of the observations or analysis source files. Rather, the *spectral object identifier* is useful to construct *links* via *direct actions* to the Spectral Object tables and the metrics recorded therein.

Spectral Inventory

Attributes of the *Spectral Inventory* Table shows whether the source is a galaxy, nebula, quasar, or late type stars as shown in (Knapp and et.al. 2006). A *direct action* constructed by *Spectral Inventory* attribute *Spectral Plate ID* can provide a *link* to the *Plate and Spectral Object Tables*. *Spectral Inventory* also contains an attribute called *MJD Combined* that appears to be the name of the plate referenced by the inventory.

Spectral Object Family of Tables

The *Spectral Object Family of Tables* are constructed to house metrics on spectral sources and observations. These tables also reference their photographic counter parts. Most of the meta-data was obtained from the data reductions for both observation types. In addition to the Spectral Object table itself, there are tables with the same attributes of sources obtained from best and target observations as shown in (Strauss and et.al. 2002). These tables have an enormous number of attributes. Subsets of these tables include a complete set of attributes to generate references to both photographic and spectral observations. Also, there are attributes to create *direct actions* to link to the plate and lines tables.

Plate Object Table

The *Plate Object Table* contains metrics of environmental conditions at the time and place where a particular spectral observation was obtained. It contains the attributes *plate id*, *MJD*, and therefore references the source file *Spectral Plate* as shown in Chapter 3 Section 3 . The *Plate Object Table* also contains the sky coordinates for the direction the telescope was pointing at the time that the observation was made. Another of this table's attributes shows the version of the IDL software described in (Hyde and Bernardi 2008) that was used to make the *Spectral Plate* source file.

Quasar Sample Object

The Quasar Sample Object as described in (Richards and et.al. 2002) is represented in the DR1 CAS by a two attribute table Best QSO (BestQSO). This table's two attributes are the identification for primary targets and object. Both can serve as references. The *primary target id* is referenced by the *Spectral Object Family of Tables*. Likewise, the *object id* is referenced by *Close*, *Lines*, *Z*, and *Spectral Object Family of Tables*. These two values provide the means to generate *direct actions* to link these tables. There are no source files that are directly referenced by the BestQSO table.

Section 2 Rule Based and Context Oriented Response Factory

In this section, an emerging technology is examined and showcased that literally uses a factory architecture governed by tasks and contexts to automatically generate a web application interface database. In exploring this concept, this work examines an example known as Direct to Web (D2W) originally produced by NeXT, refined by Apple[11], and provided as an open source product by Project Wonder. The tasks that D2W is designed for are based on an architecture known the Create, Read, Update and Delete (CRUD) shown in (Dept, Hesselink et al. 1998, Bartalos and Bieliková 2008). D2W also hinges on the ORM engine and data model described earlier in section Chapter 3 Section 2.

D2W, as illustrated in Figure 7, provides a factory, a common mechanism defined in (Gamma, Helm et al. 1994), as well as its dependencies. The set of concepts on which the D2W factory is dependent on include an *application-session context*, a set of rules, a *rule engine*, *response templates*, *attribute level components*, *component templates*, and *default behavior*. The original RIQS was implemented with this framework. At the time, the control mechanisms to make this implementation practical were not published. An examination of this framework was necessary to gain a capacity to generate query pages for every attribute in a given table, provide a meaningful listing of the query

---

[11] both NeXT and Apple are registered trademarks of Apple, Inc.

response, and an inspection of each record in DR1. In the end, D2W's dependency on the ORM both provides it the means for optimizing a database scheme and exposing poor design.

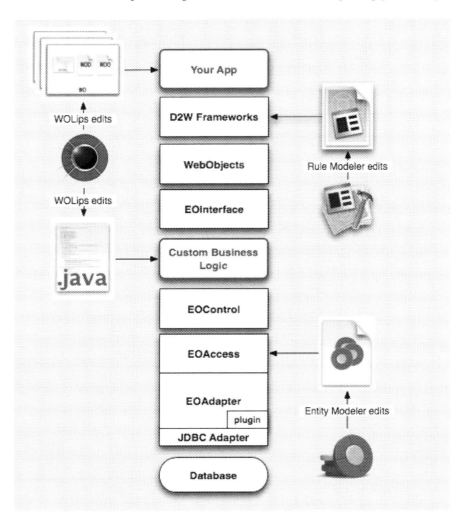

Figure 7 This diagram was taken from David Leber's World Wide WebObjects Developer's Conference (WOWODC) 2009 session on Direct to Web.

Sub-Section 1 Rules and Engines

Rule engines have been implemented in many ways such as Prolog described by (Ullman 1988, Anil Nerode 1997). Such rule engines are based on predicate logic. In the case of Direct to Web (D2W), the definition of a rule is a sentence that is composed of a *priority*, a *left hand side*, a *right hand side*, and a *type*. The *left hand side* is a conditional. The *right hand side* is an assignment. If the condition on the *left hand side* is satisfied, then the assignment on the *right hand side* is set. A *priority* is a value that determines a tie break between two rules with the same *left hand side* conditions and conflicting right hand side assignments. A *type* is the particular kind of assignment that the *right hand side* is. The syntax for a rule is defined as follows.

```
priority: leftHand => rightHandSide [type]
```

The Project Wonder version of D2W supports assignments of plist types as described earlier in Chapter 4 Section 3 Sub-Section 3 .

The rule engine is a mechanism for processing these rules and server (application) side state as shown in its primary class description[12]. The rule engine maintains state for dynamic pages, caching, rule files, collections of rules, regular and debug mode, rule order, and client configuration. It is the application-session state that is used by the factory to determine how to construct the appropriate response. The collection of rules is often called a *r*ule model.

Sub-Section 2 Context Management

Another dependency for the D2W factory is the *a*pplication - session context. The *a*pplication - session context is a collection of state to include properties from the web application, its sessions, any component contained there within, and the rule model. This collection provides *attributes, entities, property keys, page name, relations,* and *task values.* Key-value coding (KVC) compliance allows the factory to utilize the *a*pplication - session context to generate pages and determine the details and appearance of each response dynamically.

Sub-Section 3 Attribute Level Components

Direct to Web (D2W) is dependent on the web application framework that it is built on and as described in Chapter 3 Section 4 . In that framework, there is a notion of a *w*eb component. To reiterate, a *w*eb component is a MVC 3-tuple consisting of web page description, a controller, and data model. The data model for a D2W application is shared throughout the application. Each generated page is a *w*eb component. What is unique about task and context oriented response factories is the necessity for *a*ttribute level components.

An *a*ttribute level component is a *w*eb component that is referable by the rule model and has accessors for outlets *object* and *key*. Typically, any component will have properties for each dynamic sub-component declared in the web page description. Also, many attribute level components are a subclass of the custom component that provides many references to the *a*pplication - session context. The *object* and *key* reference are how the factory references the specific object and key the component is to represent. In combination with the rule model and *a*pplication - session context, this characteristic provides a dynamic mechanism to customize components not specified in the plist data structure such as images, hyperlinks, or anything that can be created for any HTML, CSS, and JavaScript oriented output.

Sub-Section 4 Default Behavior

Typically, an *a*ttribute level component is specified in one of the rule files to be used with either a type of attribute or for a particular attribute. D2W supports seven different default appearances, which are called *l*ooks. These looks are accompanied by their own rule files. These rule files provide a default set of specifications as to the appearance of each component. Each of the rules contained

---

[12] *http://webobjects.mdimension.com/hudson/job/Wonder54/javadoc/index.html?er/directtoweb/components/ relationships/package-summary.html*

in these rule files have low priority to allow for the developer to override these rules. Amongst these looks are neutral, basic, and WO look provided in the baseline WebObjects frameworks. In addition Project Wonder supplies a neutral look, an Ajax look, and Excel[13]. There are two other look currently in prototype called the "Diva" look[14], which is designed for flexibility when used in CSS customized sites or mashups, as described in (Howell, Jackson et al. 2007) and ER Modern[15].

Sub-Section 5 Flow Control

These responses are to be throttled down due to the size and composition of the catalog. This need was discovered early in the construction of the RIQS prototypes described in Chapter 3 Section 4 . The solution can be found by limiting the fetch size[16] for each table in DR1's Catalog Archive. Thus, all of DR1 becomes available in this case.

Section 3 Rule Based Request and Response

In this section, the rule based system described in Section Section 2 for generating web-pages known as Direct to Web (D2W). The responses from D2W are to be throttled down due to the size and composition of the catalog. This need was discovered early in the construction of the Revised Image Query Service (RIQS) prototypes described in (Beatty and Lopez-Benitez 2009) and Chapter 3 Section 1 . The solution can be found by limiting the fetch size[17] for each table in the Catalog Archive of the Sloan Digital Sky Survey Data Release 1 (SDSS DR1). Thus, all of DR1 becomes available in this case.

The syntax for a D2W rule set can be used to explain how to dynamically control both the query system and caching system. It is this level of control that is necessary to extend D2W's capabilities to handle large unorganized datasets.

The Object-Relational Machine (ORM) includes two caching systems. One of them is known as *b*atch display group[18]. The other caching system is the *d*efault caching system[19]. The default caching system is commonly referred to as a *b*rute force memory caching approach since it loads the entire dataset for a given query. The *b*atch display group utilizes the indexing of a given table to limit the results of a query that are stored in memory. The *b*atch display group was designed for well-organized datasets. Additional caching systems have been proposed and added to the Project Wonder version of the Enterprise Objects ORM by extending the *D*isplay Group class.

The DR1 metadata catalog is clearly not a well-organized dataset. There are tables of DR1 that do have indices, and *b*atch display group may be capable of properly caching those tables with their indices. Both caching systems are sub-systems of the ORM described in Chapter 3 Section 2 .

---

[13] Excel is a trademark of the Microsoft Corporation.

[14] Introduced at WOWODC 2009 and developed by Ravi Mendis.

[15] Introduced at WOWODC 2011 by David Leber who also developed it with funding from Apple, Inc.

[16] http://wiki.objectstyle.org/confluence/display/WO/D2W+Flow+Control

[17] http://wiki.objectstyle.org/confluence/
display/WO/D2W+Flow+Control

[18] The batch caching system is implemented by the *E*RXBatchingDisplayGroup class.

[19] The default caching system is implemented by the *W*ODisplayGroup class.

Both cache systems have attributes that can be set by the rule based system. Certain attributes are more applicable for some tables and not others. The rule based system provides a clean mechanism of determining which condition exists, and allowing the context manager described in Chapter 3 to auto-generate query, list, or inspection pages even for tables with 700 attributes or more.

The rule set in Listing 1 will turn off the *batch* display group. This listing contains two rules. In the first rule, the priority is set to *1*. Priorities are subset of natural numbers that rank rules. The tie break between two rules with the same left hand rule and conflicting right hand rules is determined by the greater priority. Therefore an applicable rule of priority 2 or greater will override this rule. This rule's left hand side is set to *true*. The value *true* is a constant and always evaluates to true. Therefore, this rule's right hand side will fire. On the right hand side, a system attribute *use*BatchDisplayGroup is set to false. If the system attribute *use*BatchDisplayGroup is false, then the default cache system is the only cache system left to use. The second rule also has a priority of 1, and has the left hand side set to the constant *true*. In this case, the right hand side is setting the system attribute of *fetch*Limit to 20. In this case, the query system attribute for *fetch*Limit is set to 20. The effect of this setting is shown in the experiments.

```
1 : *true* => useBatchingDisplayGroup = false
  [BooleanAssignment],
1 : *true* => fetchLimit = 20
  [Assignment],
```

Listing 1 Brute Force Loading Rules Group

The first of two rules in Listing 2 has a priority of 150, and a left hand side set to the constant *true*. In this case, the right hand side is setting the system attribute of *use*BatchingDisplayGroup. This is supposed to tell the ORM to use *batch* display group as the caching system. The second rule has a priority of 160 and is set to the constant *true*. In this cases, the system attributes of *batch*Size is set to 5. This attributes are supposed to set the number of records displayed by the cache system to five.

```
150 : *true* =>
    useBatchingDisplayGroup = true
  [BooleanAssignment],
160 : *true* => batchSize = 5
  [Assignment]
```

Listing 2 Batching Display Group

The rule system can also affect the query system by determining which attributes to search for. For example, Listing 3 has a priority of 160. The left hand side evaluates whether the *entity* being examined is named *Best*TSField. If the *entity* being examined is named *Best*TSField, then rule engine evaluates if the current *task* is a *list* or *query*. If the current page to be displayed is a list page or query, then this evaluation is also true. Under those conditions, the right hand side of the rule fires. The right hand side sets the *d*isplay Property Keys for the query or list page to *run*, *rerun*, *camera* column, and *field*.

```
160: entity.name='BestTSField' &&
    (task='list' or task='query') =>
    displayPropertyKeys = (
        run,
        rerun,
        camcol,
        field
    );
```

Listing 3 Batching Display Group

The rule listed in Listing 3 Batching Display Group is useful in limiting attributes in the *query*. For example, the *S*pectral Object Family has nearly 700 attributes. It should be noted that the Direct to Web (D2W) framework used to implement this work comes prepackaged with large quantity of rules. These rules may vary depending on the *l*ook being used, as described in Section 2 Sub-Section 4 . These rules are supplied by many files provided in each of the frameworks chosen by the developer. The proposed work utilizes the *E*R-Modern look for many of its rich feature set. The three listings provided in this section are both examples and samples from prototypes used to test the rule-based Revised Image Query System (RB-RIQS) concept. An ideal optimized version RB-RIQS was devised as consequence of the result from the experiments, and that version is listed in Section 5 .

Section 4 Experiments

Tests were run to compare delivery of the data from the Image Query System (IQS) metadata catalog regulated by the rule based system. The variable being tested is the choice of caching systems. The rule system can make this choice on a table by table and task by task level. Having the performance metrics of each caching system can help devise a rule set that optimizes access to this data, even if it is unorganized. These metrics also show the resources in terms of services and memory necessary to deliver these tables reliably.

Two testbed networks were used to collect metrics. In both testbeds, the client is a MacBook Pro running Apple's OSX version 10.6.6 with the Safari web browser, version 5. A small network of two nodes is used to acquire the results reported.

A public testbed network is used to collect metrics. In this testbed, the client is a MacBook Pro running Apple's OSXversion 10.6.6 with the Safari web browser[20], version 5. A small network of two nodes is used to acquire the results reported. The server (a Mac Pro[21]) is connected through the Texas Tech network (TTUnet). Whereas the client node is connected through cable modem from Ridgecrest, California.

A query with no arguments defined is called a blank query. The application presents the result of a blank query as a list of each row from the specified database table. Each test involved submitting a blank query underneath controlled conditions. This condition represents the worst-case condition for a database application caching system.

---

[20] Apple, MacBook Pro, OSX, and Safari are trademarks of Apple, Inc.

[21] Mac Pro are a trademarks of Apple, Inc.

A new version of Revised Image Query Service (RIQS) described in (Beatty and Lopez-Benitez 2009) is re-written to incorporate the rule based engine. On each testbed, a copy of the web application was installed. A rule set is devised to for each choice of caching system.

The user presents the application a blank query via a query page as shown in Figure 8. The result of a blank query (a query with no arguments) is a list of each row from the specified database table, as shown in Figure 9. Each test involves submitting a blank query underneath controlled conditions. This condition represents the worst-case case scenario for a database application caching system.

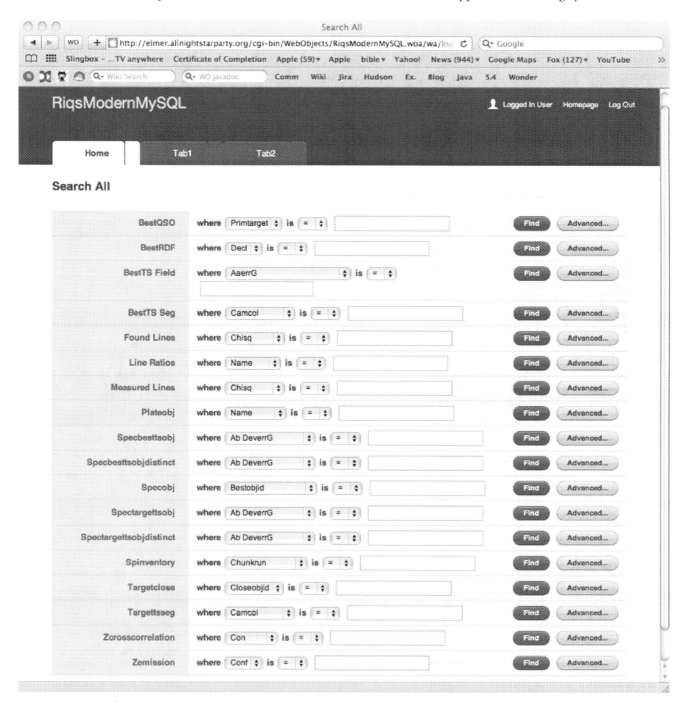

Figure 8 Rule Based Revised Image Query Service Query Page

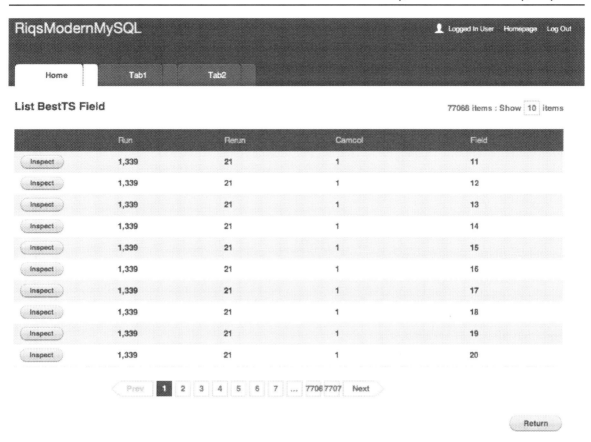

Figure 9 The Best Target Selection Field Query Result List

If the list page is loaded, then a selection for subsequent pages are selected at random for a total of three times per trial. There are ten trials for each table under each caching system. If instead presenting a listing of query results the browser times out, then the browser is refreshed when RIQS has completed the query request.

Times are recorded from Safari's development extensions that incorporate the same tools as Shark used in (Beatty and Lopez-Benitez 2009). In the event of a web browser time out, the RIQS log is used to provide the time to complete the query. Server side memory consumption are also observed in each of these tests. Memory usage are measured from the server machine using applications such as *t*op and Apple's *A*ctivity Monitor.

Once the measurements from the two experiments is acquired, a pattern is expected to emerge. If a pattern emerges, then a hybrid can be constructed that has optimized access to the metadata catalog while conserving server side memory.

Section 5 Results

There are number of categories of results. One category is the *n*early no-cache hit index error category is characterized by the batching display group nearly always having a zero cache hit. The second category of results can be called a *m*iss-and-hit. The third category is a *nearly-always-hit*. Each category should be considered in devising a hybrid system for such a category.

The tables that fit in the first category of *nearly* no-cache hit index error include *Best* TS Segment, *Target* TS Segment, *Found* Lines, *Line* Ratios, *Measured* Lines, and *Z* correlation. As such, an error type called an *out* of bounds error occurs frequently. In these cases, less than 1 out 28 attempts actually allow for the system to obtain a cache hit and present the data. This trend is shown in Figure 10 for the *Measured* Lines table.

The first measurement in Figure 10 shows the time required on average to load a set of *measured* lines under the *batch* display group. *Measured* lines are in the *nearly* no-cache hit index error category and Figure 10 shows that the report of the cache miss is relatively quick. The next are measurements for reload attempts. On rare occasion, a hit actually does occur. The fourth measurement is for a query under the choice of the default. In this case, the first query causes the cache system to load the entire table into memory. The memory footprint for this table averages out to 800 MB. The time required to load the table into memory exceeds the time out for the browser. The D2W application provides the query response on average in less than seven seconds. Subsequent requests for listing pages of the measured lines table require under four seconds to load. This example shows the excessive time required to load such a table. The measured lines table is a medium size table. However, its inability to use the *batch* display group caching system severely limits any efficiency that can be imposed. A similar pattern is shown for the *Line* Ratios in Figure 11. The default caching system's tendency to load the entire table is what leads to the other name for the default caching system, *brute* force memory-load caching system or simply *brute* force.

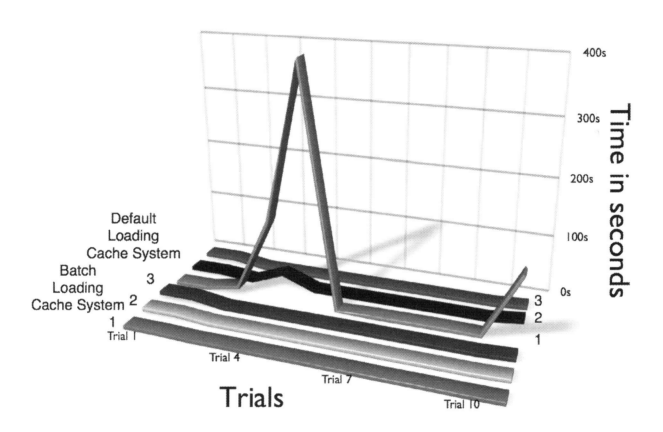

Figure 10 Brute Force Memory Load Delivery Times for the Measured Lines from selected trials.

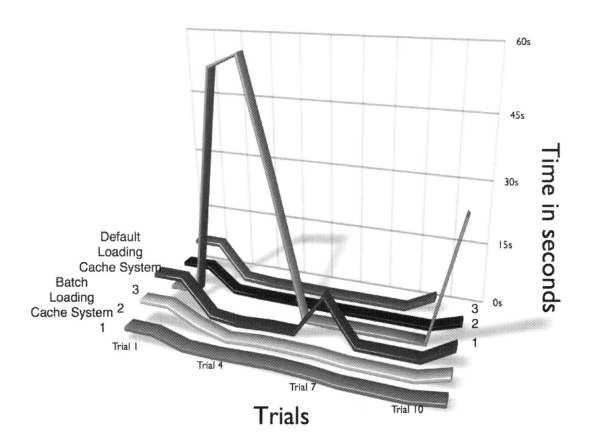

Figure 11 Load Times for the Table Line Ratios from selected trials

The second category (*miss-and-hit*) of fault failure occurs for Spectral Best Target Segment Object, Spectral Object, Spectral Target Target Segment Object, and spectral inventory. These tables will fail on the first try, but often succeed on the second try. These are examples of cache misses due to index out of bound errors. Unlike the first case, these almost always recover so that a browser refresh will obtain the data. This trend is shown in Figure 12.

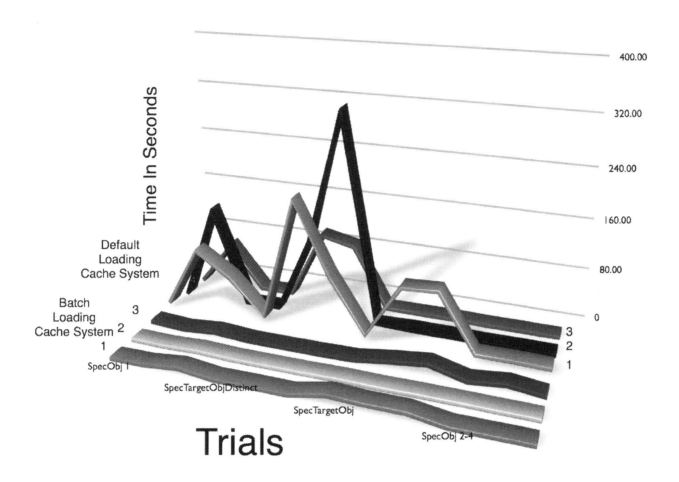

Figure 12 Spectral Object Times

In the category of *m*iss-and-hit, the brute force memory fetching can overcome the cache miss deficiency, but at a cost of keeping the data resident in memory. The column for *m*emory loading 1 shows that the default caching system has a trend to cause the first query to fail as it takes from a minute to about four minutes to load into memory. This load also presumes that adequate memory exists. After this load, queries take less than one half of a second, as shown for *m*emory load 2 and *m*emory load 3.

Loading memory by brute force is cumulative. Therefore, if more than one table is given a blank query, then both tables will occupy memory to cache it for present and future requests. The maximum table memory footprint observed has been 6GB in the case of Spectral Target Object Distinct, but this outlier is not shown in Figure 13. Figure 13shows the next largest have a memory footprint of 1 to 5 GB on average. This large footprint occurs mostly for the Spectral Object family and Z-Correlation. Since this effect is cumulative, a few of those tables combined have been observed to cause an out of memory failure. An *o*ut of memory failure causes the process to crash, the system will kill the process, and if recovery is set then restart the process. The restart in effect clears the cache. Therefore, a sufficient amount of memory must be allocated in the case of providing these larger tables where the choice of *b*atch display group will not work.

Figure 12 and Figure 11 shows that a trade-off does exists. Figure 12 shows that there is a cost in the form of high memory consumption for choosing the default caching system. In the case of *b*atch display group, cache misses that occur and tend to be less pronounced since they can be recovered from. The *b*atch display group cache misses are more frequent. The memory footprint was observed to be less than 200MB for queries using the *b*atch display group.

Some tables exhibited *n*early no cache hit index errors and the time required for a query result to load could be as much as two minutes. In most cases, the response is within a second. In the case of the *m*iss-and-hit, both hits and misses typically occurs within a second or less.

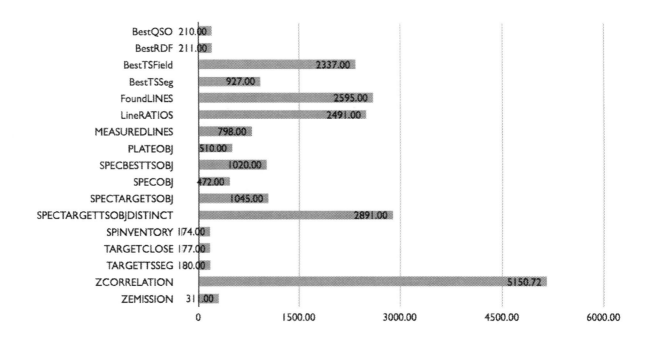

Figure 13 Memory Footprint

A case exists for the choice of the *b*atch display group in the case of *n*early-always-hit. While it may not make much of a difference in time to deliver content, it does make a difference in conserving server memory. Trials for *b*atch display group with the *n*early-always-hit have some outliers of 1.8 and 8.4 seconds. These outliers occurred in less than one out of nine cases. Otherwise, trials for *b*atch display group for the *n*early-always-hit have query and retrieval speed on the order of $1/10^{th}$ to $1/100^{th}$ of a second.

The one characteristic not tested in this work is the use of the load balancer provided by the WebObjects Task Manager. It is unknown to this work if the brute force memory loading footprint would be distributed amongst the nodes involved in such a load balancing scheme.

CHAPTER 6

REPRESENTATIONAL STATE TRANSFER ARCHITECTURE

One of the challenges of content delivery inherent with Data Release 1 (DR1) and subsequent releases by the Sloan Digital Sky Survey (SDSS) is common amongst the collection metadata catalogs in use today. Many metadata catalogs have a feature of schema and table bloat in (Cole 2007, Steward P. MacLeod and et.al. 2008) that were never revised due to the intense demand for the data that they contain. Whatever the reason for this phenomenon, the consequence is that metadata catalogs that are in use require huge amounts of maintenance to ensure their continued functionality and are in danger of collapse. When these services collapse, the software providing these services either falls into obsolescence or is simply lost. So long as the database itself exists, work reported in (2009, Beatty and Lopez-Benitez 2010, Beatty and Lopez-Benitez 2011)describe a new interface approach that can be constructed for that data.

The work reported in this chapter describes procedures and capabilities to transform that data from unorganized and unwieldy structures into a scalable, organized, efficient repository. Such a repository is ideal for mobile and cloud applications where the repository is composed of many cloudlet repositories and the joining of data occurs in a mashup, a mobile application, and/or a grid job. These capabilities yield better flexibility, improved image description, a more selective image retrieval, better tabular data recall, and faster query response time.

Section 1 A Model for Photographs Taken By Spectroscopes

Chapter 5 Section 1 Sub-Section 1 showed a query service description that includes spectral observations, photographic observations, and the metadata tables collected. Chapter 2 Section 1 reviewed the domain necessary to construct the notion of Spectral Observations (SO). This section shows how to construct an internet Flexible Image Transport System (iFITS) with SO from an an observation centric data model described in (Beatty and Lopez-Benitez 2010) for an astronomical catalog of photographic observations.

Sub-Section 1 Spectral Domain Model

The spectral domain obtains observations typically using plates with arranged fiber optics. These fiber optics attempt to isolate source objects. There are further attempts to isolate sources from bias, noise, and other unwanted sources. Thus let a Spectral Observation (SO) be defined as follows:

$$SO = O \cup \{SC, N, SB, SA^*\}$$

Equation 18

where N is a descriptor of the instrument, SB is a bundle of spectral observations, and SA^* is a set of articles contained in the spectroscopic observation. Note that N is made abstract so that descriptions of the instrument can evolve to include plated and non-plated spectroscopes in future designs.

Let a Spectral Bundle, SB, be defined as follows:

$$SB = \{n, SO^*, G^*\}$$

where SO^* is an array of SO, G^* is an array of collection graphs, and n is the name of the collection.

Let SA be defined as follows:

$$SA = \{PL, SO, SL, DR^*, n\}$$

where PL is the plate location, SL is the sky location, DR^* are data reductions, n is the name of the object, SO is as defined in Equation 17.

Sub-Section 2 Joining the Photographic Model

Both Photographic Observations (PhO) and SO are both telescope observations, O, as defined in Equation 5. Since the source FITS image is common to both, O may be rewritten as follows:

$$O = \{d, s, v, u\}$$

where d is the date, s is the site where the observation was made, v is a version string to distinguish multiple observations from the same site at the same time, and u is the URL of the source file of the observation. An illustration of the derived objects is found in Figure 13

Next, let a PhO be rewritten as follows:

$$PhO = O \cup \{\lambda, PhA^*, PhB\}$$

Equation 19 Model Re-Write Observation

where λ is the wavelength of the filter used on the PhO, PhA^* is an array of photographic articles, and PB is a photographic bundle referencing previews and a collection of PhO.

Similarly, let SO as shown in Figure 13 be defined as follows:

$$SO = O \cup \{N, SA, SB, SR\}$$

Equation 20 Spectral Object Refined

where N is the a name or description of the instrument that acquired the observation, SA^* are the articles that were observed, SB^* is an array of spectral argument, and SB is a bundle of spectral observations.

Let a bundle be defined as a collection of observations that may have analysis in common. Therefore, let a bundle, B, as shown in Figure 13 be defined as follows:

$$B = \{n, C^*, O^*, \overline{Pr}\}$$

where n is the name of the bundle, C^* is an array of calibration analysis, O^* is an array of observations, and $\overline{Pr}$ is an array of previews.

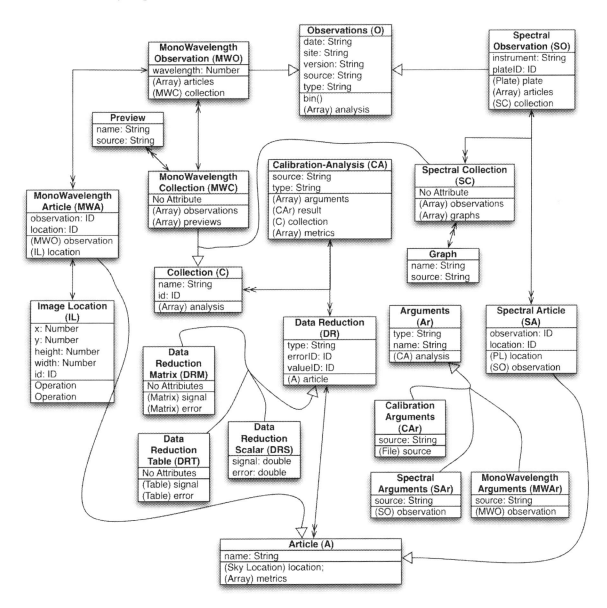

Figure 14 iFITS with Spectral Observations

Let a source article, A, as shown in Figure 13 be an object in the night sky such as a star, nebula, quasar, galaxy, and etc defined as follows:

$$A = \{n, SL, DR^*\}$$

where n is the name of the source, SL is the sky location, and DR^* is an array of data reductions.

Let a Photographic Article, PhA, as shown in Figure 13 then be defined as follows:

$$PhA = A \cup \{PhO, IL\}$$

where PhO is as defined in Equation 16 and IL the location of the source in the PhO.

Similarly, let a Spectral Source, SA, as shown in iFITS with Spectral Observations
be defined as follows:

$$SA = S \cup \{PL, SO\}$$

where SO is as defined in Equation 17 and PL is the location in the plate used to make the SO. Calibration Analysis (C) is special in their own respects. A C has a link to a bundle and that is how such a bundle keeps track of the various calibrations done on its collection. Note that C may be sub-classed to include multiple types calibration engines such as Dervish or FITSIO derived engines such as DS9 and IRAF.

Let a C as shown in Figure 13 be defined as follows:

$$C = \{n, s, B\}$$

where n is the name of the calibration, s is source of the executable to generate the calibration, and B is the bundle that owns the calibration.

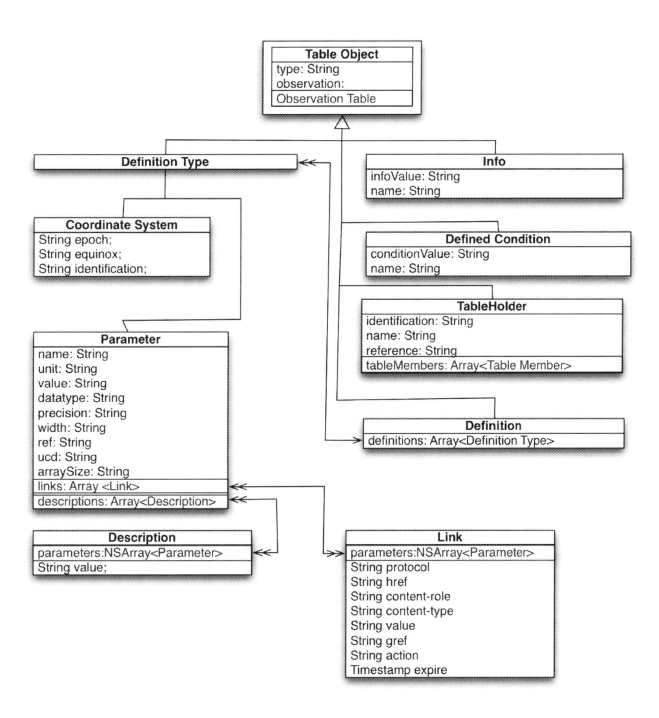

Figure 15 Non ORM friendly Version of Table Object

Section 2 Dynamic Tabular Data About The Night Sky In A Relational Database

Sub-Section 1 Object-Relational Friendly Virtual Observation Tables

In addition to storing spectral and photographic observations, there is a clear need to store tabular data. This concept has been formulated as the Flexible Image Transport System (FITS) (Wells, Greisen et al. 1981, Center 1995) in the late 1970's. The Virtual Observatory (VO) introduced the notion of a XML scheme called the VO Table. The VO Table structure offers many of the features of the FITS format, except image storage.

The VOTable schema, shown in Figure 14, is not an ORM friendly structure. Typically, an ORM can deliver any structure a RDBMS can provide. What makes a database scheme ORM friendly is the absence relationships that produce unresolvable faulting and ambiguity. For example, suppose that a class such as *Definition Type* has an one to many relationship with the class *Definition* ($\mathcal{F}$). If an object of ($\mathcal{F}$) were to fetch the attribute *d*efinitions the expected response is to return an array containing objects of class *Parameter* ($\mathcal{P}$) and *Coordinate System* ($\mathcal{X}$). The Figure 14 shows that this relationship is a one to many. An ORM is supposed to translate such a fetch into a RDBMS query. Such a query produces an ambiguity that is not practical for a RDBMS to resolve.

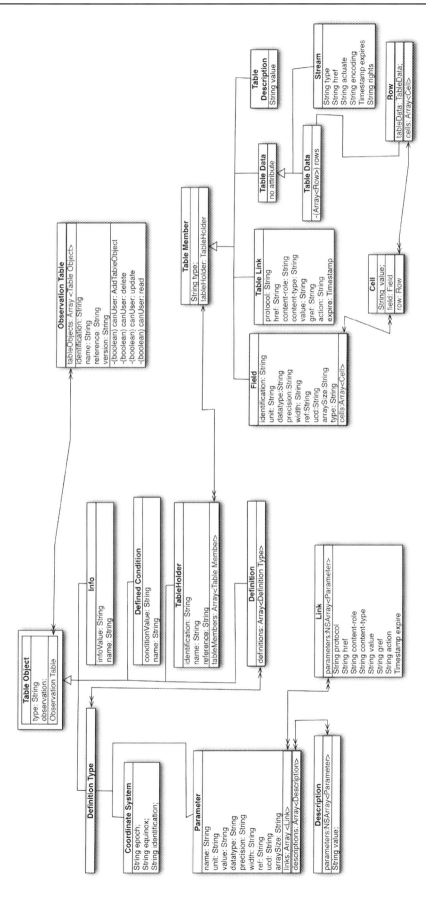

Figure 16 Tabular Observation

There is an equisatisfiable form of the VOTable schema that is ORM friendly shown in Figure 15. The object has a many-to-many relationship, and the business rules are provided validation to restrict the relation to one-to-many. The metadata section of the VOTable is loaded into a tabular observation by making each kind of table metadata at *Table Object* class. Figure 16 shows this collection includes an *Info* class $\mathcal{I}$, a *Defined Condition* class ($\mathcal{DC}$), a *Description* class ($\mathcal{D}$), a *Table Holder* class ($\mathcal{H}$), and a *Definition* class ($\mathcal{F}$). The table holder class provides reference to an array of *Table Member* classes. A *Table Member* ($\mathcal{M}$) class can be a *Table Link* (τ), *Field* (Φ), *Table Description* ($\mathcal{TD}$), *Table Data* ($\mathcal{T}$), *Stream* ($\mathcal{ST}$). There are two addition classes related to the *Table Member* classes, namely *Row* ($\mathcal{R}$) and *Cell* ($\mathcal{C}$) classes. This structure provides the basis for a dynamic table in the RDBMS that can grow as the user's needs grow.

When combined with the photographic and spectrographic observations, there is a notion to eliminate the data reduction classes in favor of using the tabular observations instead. This model is illustrated in Figure 16.

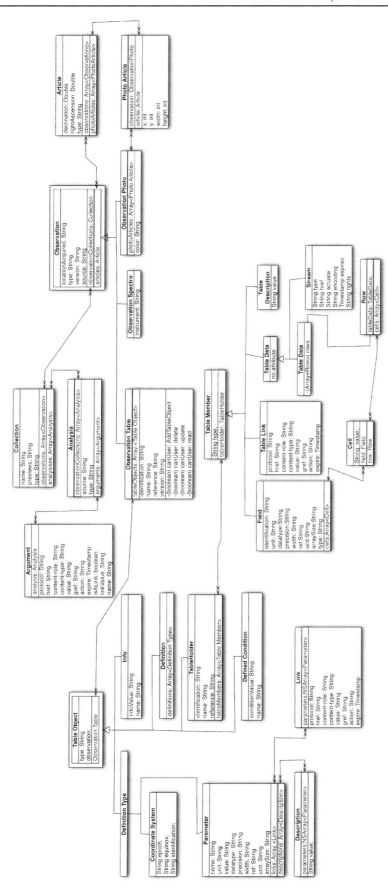

Figure 17 The iFITS Structure without Attachments

Sub-Section 2 General Table Migration

The migration process also requires a bridge to migrate IQS to iFITS in part or in full as the user sees fit. Every SQL database table has the notion of a *field*. In the case of a SQL database, a *field* is a column in a table that is mapped to an ORM class attribute (*a*). This leads to a mapping of DR1 table columns to iFITS/ VO table *fields*. Furthermore, every table in DR1 can be mapped a table holder class ($\mathcal{H}$) instance referenced by a tabular observation.

For any table in DR1, let an instance, *h*, of Table Holder class ($\mathcal{H}$) be mapped as follows:

$$f_1 : (r_t) \rightarrow h(id, n, r)$$

where *id* is the identification of the table and automatically assigned by the ORM friendly VO Table, *n* is the name of the table and is acquired from the DR1 table, and *r* is set to the URL of the DR1 instance from which the table is mapped.

Now that each table of DR1 can be mapped to a table holder in a tabular observation and each field of that DR1 table can be mapped to a field contained by the table holder, any row and the cells it contains can be mapped to an instance, *r*, of a Row class (*R*) and the cells referenced by that row and corresponding ϕ (instance of the table field class ϕ).

$$f_2 : (r_t(a, g)) \rightarrow c(\phi(id = a, r(r_n)))$$

where *a* is the attribute of the DR1 table, r_t; *r* is a row instance in iFITS; r_n is the row label corresponding to the global unique identifier of an entity in the DR1 table.

Section 3 Ubiquity by Representation

A Representation State Transfer (REST) Web Service service provide a set of remote procedure calls (RPCs). Each RPC obtains the data in a formats that are neutral to the underlying DBMS. Also, each RPC has a number of common parsers in existence and the means to perform mapping such as described in (Beatty and Lopez-Benitez 2009).

Providers of REST Web Services must employ adequate query restrictions and memory to ensure that interactions are stable. The work reported in (Beatty and Lopez-Benitez 2011) and Chapter 5 provides the necessary metrics to ensure stable interactions. The pace of an RPC's request and response system must be quick for the REST Web Service to be sustained of the lifetime of the RDBMS.

The work proposed, illustrated in Figure 17, in this section includes both peer-to-peer interaction both on client/mobile and service side. This interaction involves mapping functions for both the data and the remote procedure calls. The remote calls involve mapping due to the REST web services architecture and the adding of special functions. The data itself requires mapping to render the data in such a way that it can be well organized, compared with other sources, and capable of being managed in a mobile environment.

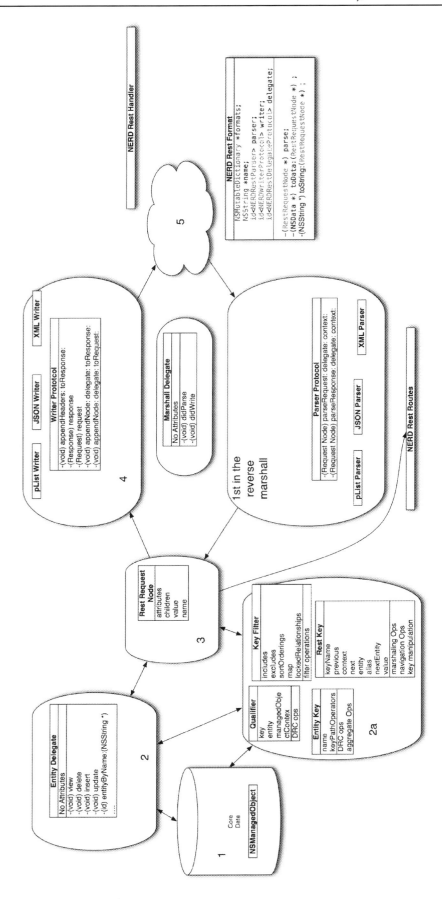

Figure 18 REST Handling and Marshaling Engine reverse engineered from the Ruby/WOnder REST engine (Project WOnder's implementation).

Sub-Section 1 Mapping Network Addresses to Survey Entities

Using the *resource-controller* architecture (RCA) described in Chapter 2 Section 4, a mapping between network address and controller-action pair can be defined. Let the resolving mapping function, *r*, be defined as follows

$$r: \{a, b\} \rightarrow \{c, d\}$$

Equation 21 Resource-Controller-Action Mapping

where *a* is the HTTP method, *b* is the resource path, *c* is a controller and *d* is a controller action. There are some conventions for predefined mappings common amongst RCA implementations. For an ORM entity *h*, let h_s be the singular name for *h* and h_p be the plural form of the name of *h*. Then Table 1 shows de facto standard value pattern for Equation 18, where *id* is global identification number for *h*.

Network Actions Mapping to Controller Actions
Table 1 Mapping Pairs

Method (a)	Resource Path (b)	Resource (c)	Action (d)
Post	$/h_p$	h_s Controller	create
*	$/h_p$	h_s Controller	index
GET	$/h_p/$id	h_s Controller	show
PUT	$/h_p/$id	h_s Controller	update
DELETE	$/h_p/$id	h_s Controller	destroy
*	$/h_p/$new	h_s Controller	new

Sub-Section 2 Another Marshaling Layer System

In order to move the data to and from the RESTful Web Service, a marshaling system is required. It is proposed that the web service application utilize an intermediary approach similar to that proposed in (Beatty and Lopez-Benitez 2009). A request node provides a basic structure of RESTful Web Service request and response envelope facilitating the construction of a simpler marshaling system. There exists an implemented framework exhibiting request node concept provided by Project Wonder[22]. Each request node is tailored for ORM structures. A set of callback methods connects each request node to other marshaling and parsing layers. Project Wonder has implemented a connection from marshaling and parsing mechanisms to fundamental data types for Project Wonder (called ERXRestFormat[23]) which includes NextStep property lists (plists) provided by the WebObjects

---

[22] http://webobjects.mdimension.com/hudson/job/Wonder/javadoc/er/rest/ERXRestRequestNode.html
[23] http://webobjects.mdimension.com/hudson/job/Wonder/javadoc/er/rest/format/ERXRestFormat.html

Foundation frameworks[24], Rails[25], and SproutCore[26] . This callback system enables the request node to acquire the marshaling capabilities from other frameworks.

Also, ORM tailored features also extend to the request node's structure. Each request node has a set of attributes and relationships that are analogous to an entity and the document types used for transport. Each node has the notion of multiple children nodes. The children node feature provides an alternative array or dictionary structure arrangement that can be used in the request and response envelop.

The request node may also implement convenience methods to convert a node into a managed/ enterprise object. These methods are based on the CRUD architecture consistent with the ORM. While these methods are convenient for the ORM, it optional for a system consuming a RESTful Web Service to implement this feature of the marshaling system.

Section 4 Migrating The Sloan Digital Sky Survey

The persistence of data is necessary for any analysis provided and sustained over time. One of the fallacies of distributed computing as documented in (Goff 2003) is that topologies do not change. Persistence providers are known to exist in the space of the cloud, mobile devices, and home devices. There are a number of techniques that facilitate the sustainment and upgrading of storage as well as link multiple sources together. In particular, there exists a technique that exports data to an external storage, establishes a new structure, and imports the data into that new structure to accommodate the new features. This technique is called *classic migration*. Web applications are beneficiaries of the techniques in the event that they utilize a persistent store capable of such transformations and there are ORM driven web applications that provide their underlying RDBMS such capabilities.

Most modern dynamic web site building frameworks include the notion of a *classic migration* process. A *migration* process establishes an instance of the RDBMS scheme and moves data from a previous RDBMS scheme instance into the new scheme instance. This process may involve many iterations.

A migration process is driven by a family of object oriented classes that have two main methods in common:

1. Upgrade
2. Downgrade

These classes are linked by a name scheme and driven by a form of Key-Value-Coding (KVC) to instantiate and utilize each of these classes methods. In order to be effective, a process may need to be dedicated to calling the proxy to perform mapping and marshaling functions.

The upgrade method maps data in the editing context and then saves that particular graph. The *migration* process includes frameworks to utilize the native language of the DBMS and it also supplies the complete EO frameworks to facilitate a notion of generic compatibility. Due to DR1's size, issues such as stability, lack of network reliability, bandwidth, latency, topology, and transport

---

[24] WebObjects Foundation and NextStep are both registered trademarks of Apple, Inc.

[25] "Rails"is a registered trademarks of David Heinemeier Hansson.

[26] http://www.sproutcore.com/

become crucial factors in this form of *m*igration process. This is why an alternative described in this section is valuable contribution.

As long as the original source exists, work described in (Beatty and Lopez-Benitez 2011) outlines an engine that dynamically constructs a new interface for that dataset. A dynamic mapping and migration provided over time and on demand may be acceptable so long as the cost of maintaining the original data source with its old structure is acceptable. When the cost ceases to be the viable, a migration of the data using the web services is an option. The same mapping functions apply to synchronizing the tabular observations with the original data source. Also, the work in Chapter 5 provides a mechanism to build an alternative migration mechanism.

This section proposes adding on to the work proposed in Section 4 by making prototypes to examine the following possibilities: proxy application to the unorganized dataset and a concept dubbed here as the synchronizing shoebox. In both cases, there is a notion of the application having a managing store and an ubiquitous active store where the data is being worked on. In the case of the ubiquitous store, access to the data is transparent and the means such as laptop, desktop, mobile device is of little relevance. In the case of the RIQS store, a read only REST Web Service is implemented with resource routes for each table in DR1, and appropriate provisions applied determined by the results in Chapter 5 .

Sub-Section 1 Proxy Application To Unorganized Dataset

The RCA architecture can be applied to the Revised Image Query Service (RIQS) proposed in (Beatty and Lopez-Benitez 2009), thereby making it a managing store. The choice of resource signatures can be arbitrary. For RIQS, it is convenient to have a resource for each table in the DR1 scheme. The actions for create, update, destroy, and new are made inert.

A proxy application is provided to access to RIQS and perform the marshaling and migration methods on the data it retrieves. This application also provides for the iFITS managing store. The proxy application needs the base URL, resources, and actions such as index and show for both managing stores. Also, the proxy application provides a mapping scheme similar to that proposed in (Beatty and Lopez-Benitez 2010). The proxy application also requires controllers to wrap around the URL-resource-action tuple to allow either a local GUI, scripting engine, or secondary program to utilize the proxy application.

Sub-Section 2 Synchronizing Application-Interface

There is a concept in REST Web Services and Recovery Services that has great potential in translating and transferring datasets. That concept is manifested as an application that subscribes and synchronizes with a class of RESTful Web Services by using a common collection of change-sets. An application of this kind is known as a shoebox application.

A shoebox application as described in (Michael E. Cohen, Jeff Bollow et al. 2007, Moxley, Kleban et al. 2008, Williams 2009, Feiler 2011) is a term describing the storage of present day digital image representations on hard drives with a digital repository analogous to previous methods of organizing photographs in shoeboxes. The concept is further refined in examples described in (Buck and Yacktman 2010, Privat and Warner 2011) as an application where each user has one standalone database instance. A shoebox application is ORM driven and each standalone database instance may collect and reference material in the file system or the database itself.

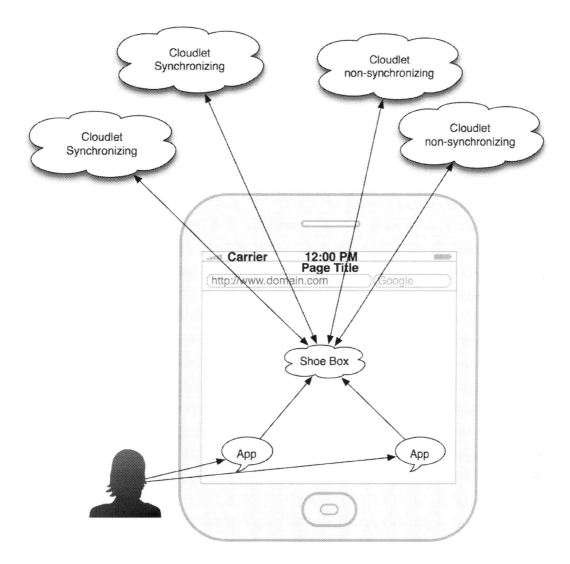

Figure 19 Mobile Shoebox application representation.

The notion proposed in this section is a shoebox application, illustrated in Figure 18, for containing and synchronizing change-sets with the following characteristics:

1. Scriptable provisions
2. A fundamental authorizer for synchronization.
3. A registration resource maintaining a set of principals binding the users, documents, services, change-sets and applications.
4. An initialization resource
5. A slow synchronization resource
6. A fast synchronization resource
7. A means to examine the change sets

8. The capability to open the application relevant to a change or registration.

9. A query manager

The application is itself is intended to be an application program interface (API) sufficient to develop and run other applications that require synchronization services, allowing the synchronization application to service many data structures other than its own.

The shoebox proposed mirrors a set of managing stores that have a special architecture for synchronizing with ubiquitous active stores[27]. We also propose this special architecture, shown in Figure 19, consisting of four main resources: *r*egistration, *i*nitialization, and *s*low change exchange and *f*ast change exchange. Let these resources operate with CRUD actions. Then *r*egistration resource provides an interface for information about a mobile/client ORM metadata. The *i*nitialization resource provides a mechanism to to obtain initial or reset state of on a mobile, remote, or peer agent from the service's source content. The *s*low change exchange and *f*ast change exchange resource is for loading and retrieving the actual data being managed.

It is proposed that this framework should be produced for the proposed iFITS with the ORM friendly VO table standard described in Section 1 and Section 2 . In this exploration, a matching mobile/ client side application facilitated by the synchronizing shoebox application is to be constructed with a migration/mapping interface between the two applications. This interface and the accompanying architecture form the basis for this kind of migration.

The *r*egistration resource processes requests for *n*ew clients. Each client is associated with *a*pplication and *d*evice shown in Figure 19. Also included in this registration is the user of the application.

The *r*egistration resource is also mirrored in the shoebox application. This resource is provided as both fundamental set of properties about a managing store, the active store application it supports, and possibly the document created by that application using the synchronized data. The shoebox application provides a MVC window or panel that provides access to every service registration the user has, with appropriate security measures imposed. The *r*egistration resource also enables the user to pull up the application associated with a particular registration. In the case of a document-based application as described in (Rassinoux, Lovis et al. 2003, Buck and Yacktman 2010), the registration is with a document that is associated with an application. There is a special marshaling structure in the case of document-based applications. Similarly, the shoebox application provide administration for the local synchronization service. The *a*pikey attribute in the *c*lient app class shown in Figure 19 is therefore used to allow for the possibility that multiple applications can access the same document.

---

[27] The ERSync framework produced by David Aspinall at Global Village Consulting and presented at the World Wide WebObjects Developer's Conference 2011 Montreal, OT Canada

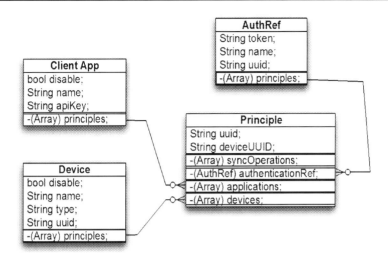

Figure 20 Structure for a Registration Resource

An *i*nitialization resource is called to start a synchronous connection between the managing store and active store applications. There are two sets of actions honored: *i*ndex and *f*ull. The *f*ull action is a special kind of *i*ndex action. The *i*ndex supplies a list of the entity objects that the user is authorized to synchronize with. This enables a synchronization list to be constructed.

The shoebox application also contains an *i*nitialization resource that is a counter part to the RESTful Web Service. For synchronization aware applications, this resource is provided as a controller interface. The synchronizing shoebox application also provides a MVC interface, such as initialize and reset button, for each registered application.

Both the *s*low change exchange and *f*ast change exchange resource contain contains a *f*ull update action. The *f*ull update action differs between the two resources by necessity. Each exchange action provides an option for different client applications to choose the methodologies best suited to their needs. In both cases, the client's push of change-set information is acquired from the intermediate marshaled state available through the request node. The processing of the pushed request node is outlined in Figure 20. A similar control and resource exists in the shoebox application.

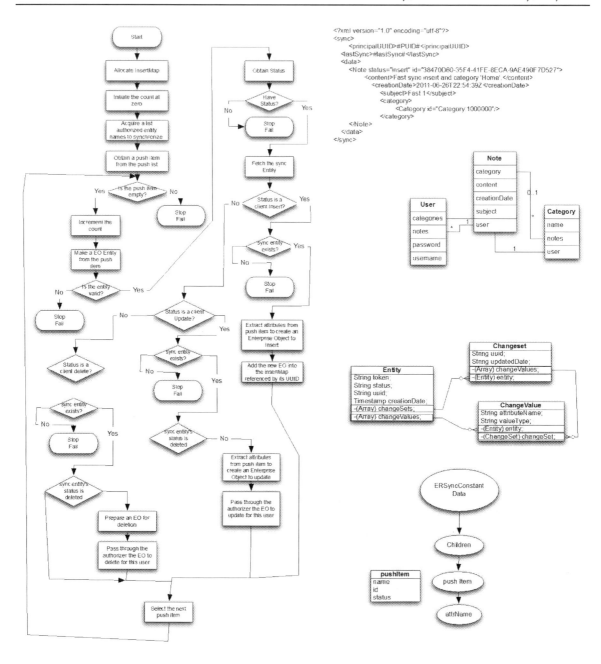

Figure 21 Process for retrieving pushed request nodes

The *full* update action for the *slow* change exchange is illustrated in Figure 21. After processing the pushed change-sets, the *full* update action looks up the list of authorized entity names to be synchronized. This is a security precaution to ensure some portions of the cloud service remain under the control of the managing store provider itself. The next step involves an arduous loop obtaining change entities from the authorized list that have changes since the last update, which is maintained in the registration information. These change-sets are loaded into the data synchronization portion of the request node to be marshaled and sent back to the user. Once all of the change entities are accounted for, the principal for this device and user synchronizing is updated, and added to the request node. The request node is then marshaled and sent back to the user as the pull data request node. The *fast* change exchange has a similar process. What distinguishes the fast and slow change exchanges in the inner loop shown in Figure 21. The *fast* change exchange establishes a query for the changes for a particular entity, as opposed to obtaining an enterprise object for the entity name. Then the *fast* change exchange filters out the changes in the list that were not made since the last synchronization process. This acquisition of just deltas is presumed to provide the speed advantage over the *slow* change exchange. A similar control and resource exists in the shoebox application. Since the project is open source, there is opportunity to add resource routes that have different characteristics to apply for different network channel conditions.

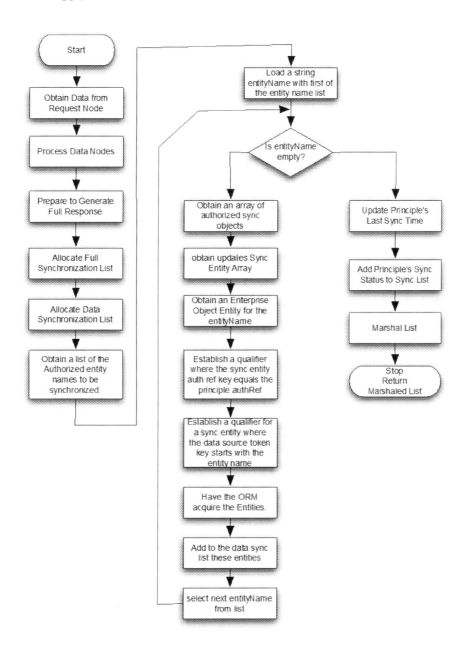

Figure 22 Full Update Action for the Slow Change Exchange

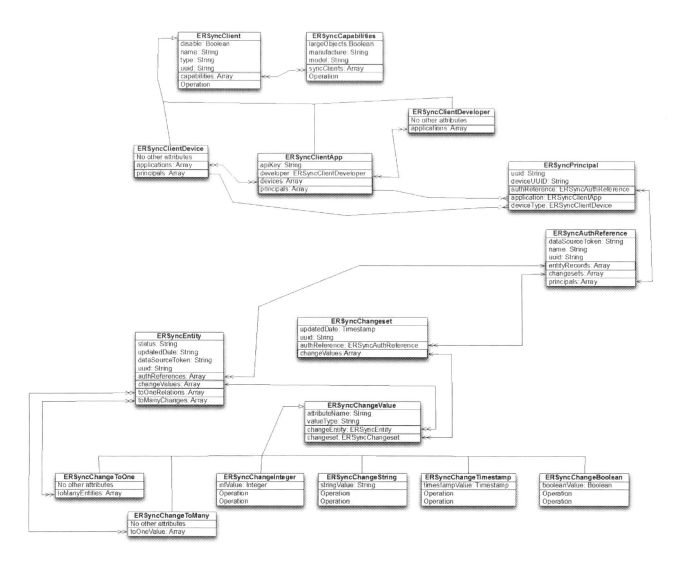

Figure 23 Model for Synchronizing Change Sets

Both the synchronizing shoebox application and managing store synchronizing architecture share a structure shown in Figure 22. In particular, the ERSyncEntity contains an attribute named *d*ataSourceToken. This token derived from marshaling the entity name and primary keys of the managed object/ enterprise object represented. This scheme serves two purposes. One, it allows the both represented object and changesets associated with the data source token to be found quickly. Two, it allows a cross reference to the attribute *u*niversal-identity (uuid). The *u*uid is intended to be unique amongst all parties conducting synchronization, which is achieved by negotiation between mobile agents and service peers. Whereas *d*ataSourceToken is specific to the synchronization registry local to the data store.

CHAPTER 7

CONCLUSIONS

We have shown evidence that given a data set, its purpose, and specific concepts (such as observations, cloud computing, and content management) that there exists an efficient structure that can be a standard for similar subject dataset(s), a mapping mechanism to incorporate these other datasets held in distinct metadata catalogs, and a virtual appliance - mashup hybrid that can automate the facade to use these disparate datasets in the same metric and scale. This was demonstrated by showing four architectures, in some cases introducing and documenting new concepts and approaches. These four architectures include: context management, mobile-code, rule-based context management, and Representation State Transfer (REST). These four architectures utilized different forms of a Revised Image Query Service (RIQS) to examine the properties of each architecture, and determine their suitability to satisfy the corollary. There were also works left for future discovery. These include tests of the REST architecture, applying load-balance to the rule-based context management architecture, and evaluate the effectiveness of the hybrid observation and table approach used by the scientist.

For example, context management system (CMS) is an architecture that governs the contributions of original, derived, or revised information components via tools that collect, analyze, revise, and organize such contributions, as explained in (Nakano 2001). Many CMS architectures require the facilities of an Object Relation Machine (ORM). An ORM's functionality is shown and documented. The value in an ORM is its ability to simplify design of data services such as RIQS. This approach reduced the amount of effort, code, and complexity necessary to obtain the Sloan Digital Sky Survey (SDSS) and enabled a fair comparison with subsequent SDSS data release.

Similarly, work on the mobile code architecture revealed an efficient structure for representing images and their transfers. This structure is called the internet Flexible Image Transport System (iFITS.) With an iFITS structure in the mobile code, it is evident that a mapping and marshaling capability does enable the presentation of the SDSS data in a more organized form. This potential also demonstrates a possibility of multiple datasets being included in the same request and response.

With the rule-based context management architecture, an automated presentation of large data sets has been devised and examined. This presentation also provides the ability to query any of the tables at the users leisure, even if the query is a blank query. This study shows the trade offs of both fault tolerance and memory caching for rule-based context management. This work elaborates the purpose of the SDSS in exquisite detail of the research performed. This work also tests cloud and ubiquitous capabilities necessary to recover full access to the catalog archive service.

With REST, the services of iFITS and RIQS were split up as two separate web services. Also, the iFITS structure was expanded to include photographic, spectrographic, and tabular observations. These tabular observations provide a version of the Virtual Observation (VO) Table that satisfies the VO specifications and the ORM's inheritance relationship requirements in a fluent way. This restructured iFITS was implemented in a rule-based context management and REST architecture.

Similarly, a synchronizing REST architecture was applied to the restructured iFITS. Lastly, the REST architecture was ported into a framework that could be made into a mobile application, grid application, and shoebox application.

There is still much to be studied and both iFITS and RIQS offer an unique opportunity for discovery. In the process of testing the RIQS to iFITS proxy, one can demonstrate the hybridization of the rule-based context management and REST. This potential exists since an iFITS shoebox enabled application could also have a web-kit interface to RIQS that can capture data, translate it, and provide that data to the iFITS service.

The REST architecture makes it possible for a proxy agent of the services to transfer data or provide an unified interface facade. In the case of a proxy facade application, this implementation could be a mobile-code agent or mobile-application. A mobile and grid application is more suitable for the data transfer application and the technique may use a selective form of migration and mapping. These capabilities present the possibility that any number of services can be called upon to provide data. In turn, the synchronizer would retain a record of each of the user's queries and results in their local copy as well as either in their private or community cloudlet. This is convenient in caching queries, synchronizing caches amongst multiple devices, and also providing a different kind of search engine. Such a search engine can reorganize the data in a form more suitable to the user's needs.

Another capability of the shoebox synchronizer that should be interesting to test is its cooperation with lateral transfer mechanisms like MPI, iCloud, and etc. The notion in this case is that the shoebox might extend the scale that MPI is currently limited to. Furthermore, this same shoebox may be capable of having greater dynamic access to mobile devices that are in use.

It is clear that this work provides the building blocks to meet the challenge of building a strong catalog. Furthermore, the architectures demonstrated indicate that a mobile connection, sharing capability, and ability to unite various datasets in a common comparison can be achieved. Therefore, this sharing can facilitate analysis on astronomical data as well as observations of other genres. Lastly, this dissertation shows that is possible to support "investigations of the distributions of luminous and non-luminous matter in the universe" and share that capability with all who endeavor to discover this knowledge.

BIBLIOGRAPHY

(2009). Image Query Service Using Content Management Techniques.

Anderson, F. (2008). Xcode 3 Unleashed, Sams.

Anderson, P. and G. Anderson (1998). Navigating C++ and object-oriented design. Upper Saddle River, NJ, USA, Prentice-Hall, Inc.

Anil Nerode, R. S. (1997). Logic for Applications. 175 Fifth Avenue, New York, NY 10010 (USA), Springer.

Armbrust, M., A. Fox, R. Griffith, A. D. Joseph, R. Katz, A. Konwinski, G. Lee, D. Patterson, A. Rabkin, I. Stoica and a. M. Zaharia (2009). Above the Clouds: A Berkeley View of Cloud Computing, UC Berkeley Reliable Adaptive Distributed Systems Laboratory.

Armour, F. and G. Miller (2001). Advanced Use Case Modeling: Software Systems, Addison-Wesley Professional.

Aronsson, L. (2002). "Operation of a Large Scale, General Purpose Wiki Website." Proceedings of the 6th International ICCC/IFIP Conference on Electronic Publishing: 27-37.

Ashford, A. R. (2006). "Celestron CPC 800 GPS." Sky and Telescope.

Aucouturier, J.-J. and F. Pachet (2002). Scaling Up Music Playlist Generation.

Bachle, M. and P. Kirchberg (2007). "Ruby on Rails." IEEE Software 24: 105-108.

Barla, M., P. Bartalos, M. Bieliková, R. Filkorn and M. Tvarozek (2007). Adaptive portal framework for Semantic Web applications. AEWSE. S. Casteleyn, F. Daniel, P. Dolog et al., CEUR-WS.org. 267.

Bartalos, P. and M. Bieliková (2008). (S)CRUD pattern support for semantic web applications. SOFSEM (2). V. Geffert, J. Karhumäki, A. Bertoni et al., Safarik University, Kosice, Slovakia: 10-21.

Beatty, D. and N. Lopez-Benitez (2009). "A Data Model for a Mobile Image Query Service." Mexican International Conference on Computer Science 0: 119-126.

Beatty, D. and N. Lopez-Benitez (2009). "Image Query Service Using Content Management Techniques." Information Technology: New Generations, Third International Conference on 0: 1335-1340.

Beatty, D. and N. e. Lopez-Benitez (2010). Mobile Metadata for Web-Based Image Query Services. MDM '10: Proceedings of the 2010 Eleventh International Conference on Mobile Data Management. Washington, DC, USA, IEEE Computer Society: 53--58.

Beatty, D. D. and N. Lopez-Benitez (2011). Rule-based Management of Large Unorganized Data Sets.

Bekki, K., W. J. Couch, Y. Shioya and A. Vazdekis (2005). "Origin of E+A galaxies: I. Physical properties of E+A's formed from galaxy merging and interaction." MON.NOT.ROY.ASTRON. SOC. **359**: 949.

Berriman, G. B. a. G., Steven L. (2011). "How Will Astronomy Archives Survive the Data Tsunami?" Queue **9**(10): 21:20--21:27.

Brandon, J., Daniel (2002). "Crud matrices for detailed object oriented design." J. Comput. Small Coll. **18**(2): 306--322.

Briukhov, D. O., L. A. Kalinichenko and et.al. (2005). "Information Infrastructure of the Russian Virtual Observatory (RVO)." IPI RAN: Moscow.

Buck, E. and D. A. Yacktman (2010). Cocoa Design Patterns, Pearson Education, Inc.

Butler, M. (2005, May 22, 2008). "Building Cocoa-Java Apps with Eclipse." from http://www. macdevcenter.com/pub/a/mac/2005/04/22/eclipse.html.

Cashion, T. (2007). Rails refactoring to resources: using crud and rest in your rails application, Addison-Wesley Professional.

Center, N. G. S. F. (1995). Definition of the Flexible Image Transport System (FITS). Greenbelt, MD 20771, NASA Goddard Space Flight Center.

Chervenak, A., E. Deelman and et.al. (2003). "High-performance remote access to climate simulation data: a challenge problem for data grid technologies." Parallel Comput. **29**(10): 1335--1356.

Cole, T. W. (2007). Proposal for IMLS Collection Registry and Metadata Repository.

Cooke, D. E. (2003). A Concise Introduction to Computer Languages: Design, Experimentation and Paradigms, Brookes/ Cole A Division of Thomson Learning, Inc.

Croft, S., W. de Vries and R. H. Becker (2007). "Radio AGNs in 13,240 Galaxy Clusters from the Sloan Digital Sky Survey." \apjl **667**: L13-L16.

Cuevas-Vicenttin, V., G. Vargas-Solar, C. Collet and P. Bucciol (2009). "Efficiently Coordinating Services for Querying Data in Dynamic Environments." Mexican International Conference on Computer Science **0**: 95-106.

Cutri, R. M., M. F. Skrutskie, S. van Dyk, C. A. Beichman, J. M. Carpenter, T. Chester, L. Cambresy, T. Evans, J. Fowler, J. Gizis, E. Howard, J. Huchra, T. Jarrett, E. L. Kopan, J. D. Kirkpatrick, R. M. Light, K. A. Marsh, H. McCallon, S. Schneider, R. Stiening, M. Sykes, M. Weinberg, W. A. Wheaton, S. Wheelock and N. Zacarias (2003). 2MASS All Sky Catalog of point sources.

Datta, D. (2002). Managing Metadata. ISMIR.

Deelman, E., Kesselman and et.al. (2002). GriPhyN and LIGO, Building a Virtual Data Grid for Gravitational Wave Scientists. HPDC '02: Proceedings of the 11th IEEE International Symposium on High Performance Distributed Computing. Washington, DC, USA, IEEE Computer Society: 225.

Dept, W. H., W. H. Hesselink, J. F. Groote, W. H. Hesselink and J. F. Groote (1998). Waitfree Distributed Memory Management by Create, and Read Until Deletion (CRUD).

Dewsbury, R. (2007). Google Web Toolkit Applications, Prentice Hall.

di Cicco, D. (2006). "ZenithStar 66 Refractors." Sky and Telescope.

Feiler, J. (2002). Building WebObjects 5 Applications, McGraw Hill/ Osborne.

Feiler, J. (2011). Sams Teach Yourself Core Data for Mac and iOS in 24 Hours, Sams.

Fielding, R. T. (2000). Architectural Styles and the Design of Network-based Software Architectures, University of California, Irvine.

Fielding, R. T., D. Software and R. N. Taylor (2002). "Principled Design of the Modern Web Architecture." ACM Transactions on Internet Technology 2: 115--150.

Fielding, R. T. and R. N. Taylor (2000). Principled design of the modern Web architecture. ICSE '00: Proceedings of the 22nd international conference on Software engineering. New York, NY, USA, ACM: 407--416.

Fogarty, J. and S. E. Hudson (2003). GADGET: a toolkit for optimization-based approaches to interface and display generation. UIST '03: Proceedings of the 16th annual ACM symposium on User interface software and technology. New York, NY, USA, ACM: 125--134.

Forcier, J., P. Bissex and W. Chun (2008). Python Web Development with Django, Addison-Wesley Professional.

Galbraith, B., P. Maric, J. Hopkins, J. Flowers, G. Frederico and P. Wetter (2001). Professional WebObjects with Java. Birmingham, UK, UK, Wrox Press Ltd.

Gamma, E., R. Helm, R. Johnson and J. M. Vlissides (1994). Design Patterns: Elements of Reusable Object-Oriented Software, Addison-Wesley Professional Computing Series.

Geer, D. (2006). "Will software developers ride Ruby on Rails to success?" Computer **39**(2): 18 - 20.

Glikman, E., D. J. Helfand, R. L. White, R. H. Becker, M. D. Gregg and M. Lacy (2007). "The FIRST-2MASS Red Quasar Survey." \apj **667**: 673-703.

Goff, M. (2003). Network Distributed Computing: Fitscapes and Fallacies, Prentice Hall Professional Technical Reference.

Goto, T. (2005). "266 E+A Galaxies Selected from the Sloan Digital Sky Survey Data Release 2: The Origin of E+A Galaxies." MON.NOT.ROY.ASTRON.SOC. **357**: 937.

Grossman, R. L., Y. Gu, M. Sabala and W. Zhang (2008). "Compute and Storage Clouds Using Wide Area High Performance Networks." ArXiv e-prints.

Gunn, J., M. Carr, C. Rockosi and M. Sekiguchi (1998). "The Sloan Digital Sky Survey Photometric Camera." Astronomical Journal **116**: 3040.

Gunn, J. E., W. A. Siegmund and E. J. M. et al (2006). The 2.5 m Telescope of the Sloan Digital Sky Survey.

Guo, R., B. B. Zhu, M. FENG, A. PAN and B. ZHOU (2008). Compoweb: a component-oriented web architecture. WWW '08: Proceeding of the 17th international conference on World Wide Web. New York, NY, USA, ACM: 545--554.

Hanisch, R. J. and et.al. (2001). "Definition of the Flexible Image Transport System (FITS)." A\&A **376**(1): 359-380.

Hanisch, R. J. and et.al. (2003). Resource Metadata for the Virtual Observatory. Astronomical Data Analysis Software and Systems. F. Ochsenbein, M. G. Allen and D. Egret. http://www.adass.org/ adass/proceedings/adass03/P3-5/. **314**.

Hayes, B. (2008). "Cloud computing." Commun. ACM **51**(7): 9--11.

Heasley, J. N. (1999). Point-Spread Function Fitting Photometry. Precision CCD Photometry. E.-R.-Craine and D.-L.-Crawford and R.-A.-Tucker. **189:** 56-+.

Hegde, S. (2004). Replication of the Data Release 1 of the Sloan Digital Sky Survey, Texas Tech University.

Hernandez, E. A. (2009). "War of the Mobile Browsers." IEEE Pervasive Computing **8**: 82-85.

Hill, C. and S. Anglin (2004). Practical WebObjects, Springer-Verlag New York, Inc (Apress) 175 Fifth Avenue New York, NY 10010.

Hillegaus, A. (2004). <u>Cocoa: Programming for Mac OS X</u>. 75 Arlington Street, Suite 300; Boston, MA 02116, Pearson Education, Inc.

Howell, J., C. Jackson, H. J. Wang and X. Fan (2007). MashupOS: operating system abstractions for client mashups. <u>HOTOS'07: Proceedings of the 11th USENIX workshop on Hot topics in operating systems</u>. Berkeley, CA, USA, USENIX Association: 1--7.

Howell, S. B. (2000). <u>Handbook of CCD Astronomy</u>, Cambridge University Press.

Hyde, J. B. and M. Bernardi (2008). The luminosity and stellar mass Fundamental Plane of early-type galaxies.

Ian H. Wittman, E. F. (2005). <u>Data Mining: Practical Machine Learning Tools and Techniques</u>. 500 Sansome Street, Suite 400, San Francisco, CA 94111, Morgan Kaufmann (Elsevier).

Jarrar, M. and M. D. Dikaiakos (2008). MashQL: a query-by-diagram topping SPARQL. <u>ONISW '08: Proceeding of the 2nd international workshop on Ontologies and nformation systems for the semantic web</u>. New York, NY, USA, ACM: 89--96.

Jiawei Han, M. K. (2006). <u>Data Mining: Concepts and Techniques</u>. 500 Sansome Street, Suite 400, San Francisco, CA 94111, Morgan Kaufmann (Elsevier).

Keidl, M. (2004). <u>Metadata Management and Context-based Personalization in Distributed Information Systems</u>, Technische Universität München.

Kifer, M., A. Bernstein and P. M. Lewis (2006). <u>Database Systems: An Application Oriented Approach</u>, Pearson Education, Inc.

Kitchin, C. R. (2003). <u>Astrophysical Technique</u>. 6000 Broken Sound Parkway NW, Suite 300; Boca Raton, Florida 33487-2742, Taylor and Francis Group, L.L.C.

Knapp, G. R. and et.al. (2006). "SDSS J103913.70+533029.7: A Super Star Cluster in the Outskirts of a Galaxy Merger." <u>The Astronomical Journal</u> **131**(2): 859-865.

Lee, C. and G. Percivall (2008). "Standards-Based Computing Capabilities for Distributed Geospatial Applications." <u>Computer</u> **41**(11): 50--57.

Lewis, H. and A. Bridger (2006). <u>GIANO: software design and acquisition facilities</u>. Advanced Software and Control for Astronomy, SPIE.

Li, K.-C., C.-N. Chen, T.-Y. Wu, C.-H. Wen and C. Y. Tang (2007). Bioportal: a portal for deployment of bioinformatics applications on cluster and grid environments. <u>Proceedings of the 7th international conference on High performance computing for computational science</u>. Berlin, Heidelberg, Springer-Verlag: 566--578.

Lindesay, A. (2008). LEWOStuff Overview, Lindesay Electronics.

Loreto, S., T. Mecklin, M. Opsenica and H.-M. Rissanen (2009). "Service broker architecture: location business case and mashups." Comm. Mag. **47**(4): 97--103.

Marinescu, F. (2006). "WebObjects to be Open Sourced; Apple to focus on WO Runtime." Info Queue.

Marshall, P. (2006). "The Hive." The Atlantic Monthly Journal.

Martinez-Medina, L. A., C. Bibineau and J. L. Zechinelli-Martini (2009). "Query Optimization Using Case-Based Reasoning in Ubiquitous Environments." Mexican International Conference on Computer Science **0**: 107-118.

Mell, P. M. and T. Grance (2011). SP 800-145. The NIST Definition of Cloud Computing. Gaithersburg, MD, United States.

Mendis, R. (2002). WebObjects Developer's Guide, Sams.

Meyer, B. (2008). "Using WebKit in your desktop application." Linux J. **2008**(171): 2.

Michael E. Cohen, Jeff Bollow and Richard Harrington (2007). Apple Training Series: iLife '08, Peachpit Press.

Moxley, E., J. Kleban and B. S. Manjunath (2008). SpiritTagger: A Location-Aware Interactive Web Tool for Annotating Your Photo Collection. Proceeding of the 1st ACM international conference on Multimedia information retrieval. New York, NY, USA, ACM: 24--30.

Nakano, R. (2001). Web Content Management: A Collaborative Approach, Addison Wesley Professional.

Nieto-Santisteban, M. i. A., A. S. Szalay, A. R. Thakar, W. O'Mullane, J. Gray and J. Annis (2005). "When Database Systems Meet the Grid." CoRR **abs/cs/0502018**.

Nowak, M., C. Pautasso and O. Zimmermann (2010). Architectural decision modeling with reuse: challenges and opportunities. Proceedings of the 2010 ICSE Workshop on Sharing and Reusing Architectural Knowledge. New York, NY, USA, ACM: 13--20.

Ochsenbein, F., P. Bauer and J. Marcout (2000). The VizieR database of Astronomical Catalogues.

Padovani, P. (1998). "The Multi-Mission Archive at the Space Telescope Science Institute (MAST)." Space Telesc.-Sci.-Inst., Newsl., Vol.-15, No.-4, p.-14 - 15 **15**: 14-15.

Paine, J. (1997). Web-O-Matic/Rexx: A tool for writing interactive Web pages that works by compiling HTML into Object Rexx. Proceedings of the 8th REXX Symposium. Heidelberg.

Pasquali, A., G. Kauffmann and T. M. Heckman (2005). "The Excess Far-Infrared Emission of AGN in the Local Universe." MON.NOT.ROY.ASTRON.SOC. **361**: 1121.

Pautasso, C. (2009). "RESTful Web service composition with BPEL for REST." Data Knowl. Eng. **68**: 851--866.

Pautasso, C., O. Zimmermann and F. Leymann (2008). Restful web services vs. "big'" web services: making the right architectural decision. Proceeding of the 17th international conference on World Wide Web. New York, NY, USA, ACM: 805--814.

Pence, W. D. (1992). FITSIO and FITS File Utility Software. Astronomical Data Analysis Software and Systems I. C. B. D.~M.~Worrall, \& J.~Barnes,. **25:** 22-+.

Pence, W. D. (1995). FITSIO Subroutine Library Update. Astronomical Data Analysis Software and Systems IV. H. E. P. R.~A.~Shaw, \& J.~J.~E.~Hayes,. **77:** 245-+.

Pordes, R., J. Trumbo, S. Veseli, M. Vranicar and H. Schellman (2001). Distributed Data Access and Resource Management in the D0 SAM System. HPDC '01: Proceedings of the 10th IEEE International Symposium on High Performance Distributed Computing. Washington, DC, USA, IEEE Computer Society: 87.

Privat, M. and R. Warner (2011). Pro Core Data for iOS: Data Access and Persistence Engine for iPhone, iPad, and iPod touch. Berkely, CA, USA, Apress.

Qiusheng, A., G. Wang and W. Zhang (2007). "The Study of Normal Form of Relational Database Based on Rough Sets Theory." Granular Computing, IEEE International Conference on **0**: 245.

Raddick, J. "Cooking with Sloan: Color-Magnitude Diagram for Galaxies."

Raivio, Y. a. L., Sakari and Juntunen, Antero (2009). Open Telco: a new business potential. Proceedings of the 6th International Conference on Mobile Technology, Application \&\#38; Systems, ACM.

Rajasekar, A., M. Wan and R. Moore (2002). MySRB \& SRB - Components of a Data Grid: 301--310.

Rassinoux, A.-M., C. Lovis, R. Baud and A. Geissbuhler (2003). "xml as standard for communicating in a document-based electronic patient record: a 3 years experiment." International Journal of Medical Informatics **70**(2-3): 109 - 115.

Richards, G. T. and et.al. (2002). "Spectroscopic Target Selection in the Sloan Digital Sky Survey: The Quasar Sample." The Astronomical Journal(123): 2945-2975.

Richardson, L. and S. Ruby (2007). RESTful Web Services, O'Reilly.

Sandoval, J. (2009). RESTful Java Web Services, Packt Publishing.

Santos, N. and B. Koblitz (2006). "Distributed Metadata with the AMGA Metadata Catalog." ArXiv Computer Science e-prints.

Shuen, A. (2008). Web 2.0: A Strategy Guide Business thinking and strategies behind successful Web 2.0 implementations., O'Reilly Media, Inc.

Steward P. MacLeod and et.al. (2008). Extending A Directory Schema Independent of Schema Modification.

Stoughton, C. (2006). "Sloan Digital Sky Survey - Data Release 1." from http://www.sdss.org/DR1/.

Stoughton, C. and et.al. (2002). "Sloan Digital Sky Survey: Early Data Release." \aj **123**: 485-548.

Strauss, M. A. and et.al. (2002). "Spectroscopic Target Selection in the Sloan Digital Sky Survey: The Main Galaxy Sample." The Astronomical Journal **124**: 1810-1824.

Szalay, A. S., J. Gray, A. Thakar, P. Z. Kunszt, T. Malik, J. Raddick, C. Stoughton and J. vandenBerg (2001). "The SDSS SkyServer, Public Access to the Sloan Digital Sky Server Data." CoRR **cs.DL/0111015**.

The SDSS collaboration (2003). "The First Data Release of the Sloan Digital Sky Survey." Astronomical Journal **126**: 2081.

Thomas, D. (2003). "The Impedance Imperative: Tuples + Objects + . . ." Journal of Object Technology **2**(5): 7-12.

Tody, D. (1993). IRAF in the Nineties. Astronomical Data Analysis Software and Systems II. R. J. V. B. R.-J.-Hanisch, \& J.-Barnes,. **52:** 173-+.

Tucker, D. L. and et.al. (2006). The Sloan Digital Sky Survey Monitor Telescope Pipeline.

Ullman, J. D. (1988). Principles of Database and Knowledge-Base Systems, Volume I, Computer Science Press.

Urban, S. E., T. E. Corbin, G. L. Wycoff, J. C. Martin, E. S. Jackson, M. I. Zacharias and a. D. M. Hall (1998). "The AC 2000: The Astrographic Catalogue on the System Defined by the Hipparcos Catalogue." The Astronomical Journal **115**(3): 1212-1223.

Vaquero, L. M., L. Rodero-Merino, J. Caceres and M. Lindner (2009). "A break in the clouds: towards a cloud definition." SIGCOMM Comput. Commun. Rev. **39**(1): 50--55.

Wang, H. and H. Fan (2009). The Research and Design of Information Sharing of GIS Based on RESTful Web Service. Proceedings of the 2009 First IEEE International Conference on Information Science and Engineering. Washington, DC, USA, IEEE Computer Society**:** 2225--2228.

Wells, D. C., E. W. Greisen and R. H. Harten (1981). "FITS - a Flexible Image Transport System." \aaps **44**: 363-+.

Williams, R. and et.al. (2004). VOTable: A Proposed XML Format for Astronomical Tables, The Strasbourg astronomical Data Center.

Williams, S. B. (2009). The Digital Shoebox: How to Organize, Find, and Share Your Photos, Peachpit Press.

York, D. G. (2000). The Sloan Digital Sky Survey: Technical Summary.

Zeng, D., H. Chen, C. Tseng, W. Chang, M. Eidson, I. Gotham and C. Lynch (2005). BioPortal: a case study in infectious disease informatics. Proceedings of the 5th ACM/IEEE-CS joint conference on Digital libraries. New York, NY, USA, ACM: 418--418.

Printed in the United States
By Bookmasters